MW00851384

TRUE PSYCHOLOGY

THE SCIENCE OF BUILDING PSYCHOLOGICAL RESILIENCE
THROUGH COGNITIVE REAPPRAISAL

GALEN E. COLE

Kiki, I'm so very proud of your service and all you do to help those who are suffering. You are amazing!

Copyright © 2015 Galen E. Cole

All rights reserved.

Table of Contents

PREFACE AND DEDICATIONS

For some strange reason, I believe it was fate, I had more than my fare share of problems growing up, including the death of my brother when I was a teenager. Fortunately, through all of my difficulties I don't recollect thinking my life was that much different or more difficult than the lives of those I grew up around.

What I do recall about my many struggles is my relentless desire to see the good in everything I was experiencing. That is, I was an optimist. This is probably because those I grew up around were some of the most pessimistic people I have ever known. For example, I recall asking my dad if he would help me pay for college. His answer was, "No, you really aren't college material, you need to learn to do something with your hands!" It was at that moment, in spite of the fact that I struggled in school and the only reason I did reasonably well was to remain eligible for sports, I decided I was going to go to college. After all, the true optimist performs best in the presence of a true pessimist. And my dad was a true pessimist. No wonder, given that he grew up in a very difficult world filled with poverty and disappointments—disappointments that only gave way to alcohol until the point in time when he learned, internalized, and began to apply the principles outlined in this book.

One problem with people being true optimists is the fact that, in spite of their positive outlook on life, bad things happen to them that can shake their sense of optimism to the core. This is especially true when bad things happen over and over again. For example, during my senior year in high school I lost the state championship in wrestling in the last two seconds of the match. And then, in college, I lost a deciding match to the national champion in my weight class in the last few seconds of the match on a technicality. Because I spent my growing up years dreaming of being a state and national champion, these losses caused me to rethink my optimism. What I discovered in this time of deep reflection is the substance of this book, which has been repeated over and over again across my lifespan.

Ironically, when I decided to write the first edition of this book, the most important underlying assumption that supports my theory of self improvement—which states that, "in case of happiness and emotional wellbeing, it's not what happens to a person, or a person's circumstances, but what they decide to think and do about what happens to them and their circumstances that counts"—was severely challenged by the deaths of my mother on March 5, 2012, my grandmother on my birthday, March 17, 2012, and my mother's brother on March 24, 2012. In keeping with what you will learn from the book, each one of these crushing losses presented me with an opportunity to become better or bitter, stronger or weaker, more or less rational. And in each instance, I made a conscious decision to become better instead of bitter, stronger rather than weaker, and more rational.

The point is that, if applied as prescribed, the "True Psychology" approach presented here will teach you how to consistently choose to use the inevitable difficulties and problems you experience in life, small or large, as opportunities for personal and interpersonal growth and development. This is not to say that I have found a new drug, supplement, or secret treatment that has just been discovered deep in the rain forest. Instead, it provides insight into the human condition and how to improve it one person at a time. The book will also help you clearly see the truth in the common laymen's definition of insanity, which is "doing the same thing over and over again while expecting a different outcome."

By using the words "True Psychology" in the title of this book, I mean that the principles discussed here can be applied at anytime in any culture with the same outcome. I know this is a bold assertion, but it's true. And, what's more important, because these ideas are based on universal truths, you can test them on yourself, in your relationships with others, in your religious practice, and at work.

I refer to the principles and ideas asserted here as "universal truths," because they apply across cultures, time periods, gender, races, and religions. For example, I discovered first-hand through my research and travels around the globe that individuals, regardless of their culture, race, or place of origin, who think negative thoughts or tell themselves irrational stories, experience negative emotions. Similarly, those who consistently treat others with disrespect eventually lose the respect of those who experience this type of treatment.

If you think about it, it's truly a good thing that there are universal truths and laws that link human behavior to certain consequences. Once you learn universal laws and decide to comply with them, you can consistently reap the consequences associated with each law. This gives predictability and a sense of certainty and control over how our lives play out. This, in turn, gives us reassurance that life isn't just a lottery or that we are simply preordained to a life that we have no control over. As any good parent or teacher or supervisor would counsel those they have stewardship over, people tend to get out of life what they put into it. Or, put another way, they tend to "reap what they sow." As you will learn from this book, this includes how you feel as an individual as well as how you tend to relate to other people and organizations.

During my developmental years I spent my summers and holidays working on my grandparents cattle ranch. We knew when it was hot we needed to check the windmills each day to ensure the cattle had adequate water. Likewise, we knew in the winter time when the temperature dipped far below freezing we would need to break the ice in the water tanks to ensure that cattle could get a drink. And, if the snow covered all the pasture forage, we needed to supplement the cows' diet with hay. We knew that if we planted a garden we had to take certain steps to ensure that we reaped the benefits of our labors. We needed to till the ground, plant good seeds, fertilize, weed, water, and protect our crops from raccoons, coyotes and deer. If we did this year after year, we always produced something that was edible.

I know all of this is somewhat elementary to the average adult, especially to those who have been around a while. What's new here is that many of those who have written about self-help psychology and how it applies to individuals and their relationships tend to leave out the part about the link between thoughts, behaviors, and consequences. This is certainly not true among those who have a true Cognitive Reappraisal approach to therapy, which includes therapies like Cognitive Behavioral Therapy (CBT), Rational Emotive Behavior Therapy (REBT), and/or Dialectical Behavioral Therapy (DBT), but it is true among many others who put up a shingle and hope to help guide their clients toward good mental health and relationships. This is because many of the theories taught in graduate school are long on best guesses and short on common sense that in many cases must be learned through experience.

My point here is that the principles, processes, and approaches outlined in this book are not simply theoretical fun and games. Rather, they are based on what leading behavioral and social scientists agree are the most important principles and conditions that must be addressed in an effective self-directed psychological change process.

More specifically, this means that learning and applying the true self-help psychology outlined here will increase your psychological resilience and overall sense of well-being by helping you understand that everyone who has a healthy brain can learn to live rationally; appreciate the fact that healthy brains have ability to change shape over time (Neuroplasticity), which translates into desirable changes in the brain that result from conscious changes in thinking (i.e., you can use your mind to change your brain for the better); understand that rational living increases happiness and emotional well-being; learn to consistently perceive yourself in a way that increases your happiness and sense of well-being; think in ways that are congruent with rational goals and a rational perception of yourself and your future—a Rational Self Perception (RSP); behave in ways that are consistent with rational goals and a RSP; develop realistic self-improvement plans that work; believe that, in the case of happiness and emotional well-being, it's not what happens to you, or your circumstances, but what you decide to think and do about what happens to you and your circumstances that counts; form a strong positive intention (or make a commitment) to make specific changes; better understand what you can do to build personal resiliency and cope in healthy, rational ways; develop basic skills, such as mental imagery and rehearsal, goal setting, resiliency development, coping, cognitive restructuring, critical thinking, self-discipline, delayed gratification, persistence, planning, and problem solving; master monitoring personal status and internal monologues to align your thoughts with your goals; gain the confidence (self-efficacy) you need to do what is required to change; understand intrinsic and extrinsic motivation and how they impact goal-oriented thinking and action; develop positive reinforcement (motivation) for doing what you plan to do; understand how to identify your triggers and overcome your barriers and tendencies to self-sabotage; believe that the advantages of doing what you plan to do outweigh the disadvantages; ensure that what you plan to do and actually end up thinking and doing is, in fact, consistent with your self-image and does not violate your personal standards; understand that setting and striving toward specific goals will give you a greater sense that life has purpose and meaning, and that achieving your personal goals will give you a discernible sense of accomplishment that is often referred to as success— the progressive realization of a worthy ideal. And, finally, this book will provide you with an appreciation of the fact that because setting and achieving goals gives a sense of purpose and feelings of success, it's rational to set and achieve goals. Conversely, not setting goals or setting goals that you don't achieve is irrational. To be rational, a goal must be specific, measurable, realistic, and stated in terms of a specific time period. In addition, you must 1) believe you can achieve the goal (have self-efficacy or confidence), and 2) actually be able to achieve it, i.e., have the required knowledge, skills, and abilities. This is because a) it's irrational to assume you can achieve a goal that you don't believe you can achieve, and b) you must become the kind of person who does the kind of things you plan to do.

Once you understand these truths you will know why people struggle as individuals and in their relationships. You will also know how to help yourself and others deal with even the most difficult problems in ways that make yourself, other individuals, and your relationships stronger. In other words, you will know how to consistently and systematically reprogram your beliefs, thoughts, actions, and how you view yourself in a way that helps you become the person you want to become, regardless of what happens to you across your life span.

To this end, I dedicate this book and the truths herein to the mostly unsung heroes across the world who get so little credit for doing so much for all of us. This includes our fighting men and women and especially my nephew Geoffrey Golden Johnson, who lost his life in Bagdad; police and firefighters like those individuals who charged in to the Twin Towers knowing that they may not come out again; helping professionals who spend countless hours trying to prevent suicide, emotional suffering, and divorce; individuals who turn their lives around and become happy and productive by over-coming crushing life events and the iron grip of addiction, like my father Edward; public health professionals who tirelessly advocate for disease prevention and health promotion; and above all, mothers and teachers, like my wife Priscilla, my mother Janice, and my grandmother Aurel, who have strong agendas for good and devote themselves to socializing healthy, rational children against great odds and for little or no pay.

INTRODUCTION

I once received a call from a person who had a serious anxiety problem. He wanted to know how much I charged for psychotherapy. Before answering and in hopes of jarring some rational thinking into his decision-making process, I asked him if he had any other criteria for selecting a therapist besides price. He said, "yes, I need someone who lives close to me." Even though I kindly suggested that he may want to ask a few more questions before making a final decision about who should help him with his problem, he continued to insist on finding the lowest priced and most conveniently located therapist. Realizing this person was not interested in the background, training, or experience of the person who would help him, I recommended that he go online and Google the phrase "cheapest therapists in Stone Mountain, Georgia" (his hometown).

Although I am not sure what he discovered, I do know that with such a limited selection criteria (cost and location), this person may have gone on to find a low cost therapist, who has an office just around the corner, and has absolutely no experience treating anxiety disorders. In fact, the cheap, conveniently located therapist may even suffer from an anxiety disorder herself. Just as not all therapist are the same, not all individuals who write "self-help books" are the same. I would hope that you keep this in mind as you look over my credentials and realize that what I have written here is not simply an exercise in theoretical fun and games. Rather, the ideas and recipes for change and personal development presented here are based on what I have discovered in my own research and clinical experience and, what other leading behavioral and social scientists agree are the most important principles and conditions that must be included in any legitimate approach to helping people better themselves, overcome troubles, improve weaknesses, and ultimately lead happier, more serene, and healthier lives.

Since I can remember, I have had a passion for helping people-my wife claims I am trying to save the world. Although it took me a while to figure out how I was going to do it, I finally landed on two approaches that have served me well. The first "world saving" idea came to me when I took an undergraduate psychology class. When I learned that there was a profession where people would pay me to help them, I was hooked. I was even more intrigued when I took my first health science class where I learned that there was a profession called public health that focused on preventing and controlling diseases among the population at large. After taking these two classes, I decided I was going to get the credentials required to work in both counseling psychology and public health. This decision has served me well in that I have spent my professional life trying to change the world one person, couple, and family at a time in my clinics, and one community and country at a time through my work in public health.

In both of my professions I have spent a considerable amount of time training other like-minded professionals. This has taken me around the world to many strange and wonderful places like Almaty, Kazakhstan; Abuja, Nigeria; Kampala, Uganda; Nairobi, Kenya; Nazareth, Israel; Cuzco, Peru; Berlin, Germany; Jerusalem, Israel; Sidney, Australia; and Bangkok, Thailand to mention a few.

The first time I really knew that I was having a broad scale impact was at a training I was conducing in Bangkok. After the training, some of the professionals who participated in my workshop asked me sit down for a special presentation. At that point they announced that a decision had been made to require all students in their last year of secondary school to use a synthetic learning support tool I was instrumental in developing, CDCynergy (Cole & Prue, 1999), to plan and evaluate their senior project. Not long after this experience I was in Beijing, China, introducing a similar learning and decision-support tool to the heads of the Chinese Centers for Disease Control—China CDC. Shortly after bringing out my learning tool, my Chinese hosts started talking excitedly among themselves in Mandarin. After going back and forth for some time, they sent a person out of the room. Shortly afterwards, this person brought back a copy of the same tool I had planned to introduce them to. To my surprise and pleasure, the Chinese had somehow gotten a copy of my tool and translated it into Mandarin.

After recognizing that my work had reached as far as China, my passion and intensity to save the world has taken on an even greater meaning and a dedication to reach as many people as I can. This has motivated me to reach out to, and begin working with, representatives of what I consider to be the most powerful channel for good or bad communication in the world, popular entertainment (Greenberg, Salmon, Patel, Beck & Cole, 2004). As you will read later on in the book, my work with writers and producers in Hollywood has allowed me to influence millions with minimal effort. It has also taught me a number of principles that I have been able to incorporate into the psychology of self-directed change techniques I will introduce later on in the book.

All said, this book is another attempt at carrying out my global mission. The book brings together the collective wisdom I have assimilated through my experience in working with different cultures regarding what it takes to motivate both individuals and large populations to eliminate unhealthy and irrational thoughts and actions and to replace them with attitudes and actions that produce rational living, increased health, happiness, and a state of serenity. In other words, it describes in some detail how "the psychology of personal resiliency and self-directed change" can help individuals, couples, and families go about systematically improving themselves and their relationships. It also describes how those who are struggling with serious problems like addiction can overcome their cravings, remain sober, and become truly happy.

Seven quotes that I have happened upon over the years have helped shape and guide what is included in this book. Each of these quotes has impacted how I think about, approach, and promote the psychology of personal resilience and self-improvement.

The first quote is credited to Steven Covey. In fact, it's the title of the second chapter in his book The 7 Habits of Highly Effective People. It simply says, "Begin with the end in mind." In keeping with this incredibly simple and, at the same time, incredibly important concept, Section I of this book provides an explanation of what I consider to be the end goal of the book, which is to persuade the reader that learning and applying the processes I introduce here, along with the accompanying psychology of change tools—referred to as Cognitive Reappraisal Techniques and taken from the fields of Cognitive Behavioral Therapy (CBT), Rational Emotive Behavior Therapy (REBT), and Dialectical Behavioral Therapy (DBT)—will help you identify and systematically go about attaining your personal algorithm for true happiness and well-being (Seligman, 2012; Rath & Hartner, 2010).

The second quote is a Turkish Proverb that says, "No matter how far you have gone on the wrong road, turn back." This quote reminds me to tell those I work with that they can, no matter how much havoc they have wreaked in their lives, change their course in life. It also reminds me to remind them that if they have gone down a wrong road for a long distance, it does take some time to get back to the right road. This truth is also evident in my the next quote.

Jim Rohn states, "You cannot change your destination overnight, but you can change your direction overnight." What this quote says to me is that a necessary first step in getting where you want to be is to make a decision to change your direction in life. Similar to the Turkish proverb I just discussed, this quote also reminds me that even though we do change course in life, it may take some time to get to our desired destination. Although individuals who do not value patience (an essential ingredient in true happiness) may not like the fact that change takes time and effort, the fact is, change does take time and effort.

The fourth quote that is fundamental to my philosophy of change is by Henry Louis Menken who once said, "There is always a well-known solution to every human problem—neat, plausible, and wrong." This quote makes the point that change is not easy and that all those who say it is don't know what they are talking about or, they are manipulating the truth as is often the case with politicians who tend to make it seem like "change" is a magical process that requires no real dedication or effort.

The fifth quote I often rely upon is by Albert Einstein who said, "Make everything as simple as possible, but not simpler." As with the Menken quote, Einstein's point here is that making things too complicated can get in the way of the primary goal, which is to give people what they need to improve without overburdening them with details.

The sixth quote by Patrick Rothfuss, in the Name of the Wind, is, "It's like everyone tells a story about themselves inside their own head. Always. All the time. That story makes you what you are. We build ourselves out of that story." This quote makes the point that what we think about ourselves matters. It matters so much that no matter how hard we try to change, we cannot change in ways that are incongruent with our self-image. Because of this, any legitimate psychological resiliency building or self-improvement approach must target the self-image.

The seventh quote I have relied on heavily in my efforts to help people improve their lives is attributed to Robert Louis Stevenson. He said, "No man can run away from weakness. He must either fight it out or perish. And if that be so… why not now, and where you stand." This reminds me to remind you, the reader, that there is no time like the present to make changes that will help you overcome weakness on the road to greater happiness.

Taken together these quotes have direct bearing on the main goals of this book. These goals are to 1) help you better understand and systematically improve your personal happiness and serenity, which is the ability to be OK when things in your life are not; 2) explain the concept and benefits of "rational living," which is the sum total of thinking and acting in ways that help you get what you want in life; 3) introduce you to 13 Competencies required to obtain and maintain psychological resilience; and 4) explain how to apply a self-directed change process that leverage these competencies in a way that will help you change whatever you want to change about yourself, including overcoming destructive habits and addictions. The contents of this book represent a serious approach to achieving these goals because it is based on proven behavioral science and neuroscience along with tried and true "recipes" that have been tested in my clinics and on large populations around the world and have proven to be universally effective. By universal, I mean these principles and processes have been effective in helping men, women, and children, of different races, from different cultures and religions, around the globe.

Section I "begins with the end in mind" by introducing you to the ultimate goal of this book, which is to help you increase your perceived happiness and overall sense of well-being. In addition to defining and explaining the construct of happiness, I introduce a conceptual tool called the "Happiness Algorithm Planner" (HAP) that you can use to 1) reliably and honestly discern your perceived state of happiness as well as increases and decreases in your happiness status, 2) isolate what makes you more or less happy, and 3) develop a plan to systematically increase and sustain your level of perceived happiness. This section also provides you with an exercise you can use to begin the process of identifying your own, unique "happiness recipe."

Section II explains and illustrates the concepts of "truth" and "rationality," in a way that will help you more readily understand, incorporate, and apply the conceptual model and principles introduced in Section III, and the 13 Competencies outlined in Section IV.

> *What we think and do determines who*
> *we are — and who we will become.*
> - Dieter F. Uchtdorf

The basic premise of this section is that everything happens for a reason. The reason we don't reach our goals is because we think and do things that do not support our goals. Conversely, when we decide to think and do rational things that support our goals, with some practical exceptions, we reach our goals. This section illustrates these points with a number of examples and stories that capture the essence of a quote by the famous American motivational speaker, Tony Robbins, when he said "Our decisions, not the conditions of our lives, determine our destiny."

What is described and diagrammatically illustrated in **Section III**, "Logic Models and Principles for Change," is presented here because I believe it's better to "teach a person to fish than it is to simply give them a fish." Accordingly, an understanding of the conceptual models introduced in this section along with the scientific principles of self-directed behavior change will help you discern, at a deep level, why the competencies laid out in Section IV are both necessary and sufficient for building psychological resilience and helping you successfully achieve your personal goals and change any behavior you are concerned about.

Section III also provides you with an extensive list of principles, assumptions, and conditions required to understand the scientific basis of happiness, psychological resilience, and self-directed change. These ideas are what differentiate this approach from other self-help books that are not grounded in clinical experience and/or empirical evidence.

Section IV introduces you to 13 Competencies that are required to obtain and sustain psychological resilience. The competencies included in this section include how to 1) measure and monitor your psychological status; 2) communicate effectively; 3) rationally define and solve problems; 4) develop and implement a personal improvement plan; 5) create a personal vision (Rational Personal Vision Statement) of what you want to BE (calm, successful, thin, on time, confident, faithful, disciplined, fun, trustworthy, etc.), DO (graduate from college, get married, travel around the world, write a book, etc.), and GET (a new car or home, great job, a boat, etc.) in life; 6) set and achieve rational goals that support your vision; 7) determine what will motivate you to change and grow; 8) identify and anticipate triggers and barriers to change and growth; 9) create a Plan of Action; 10) mentally program and internalize your RPVS, goals, and Plan of Action by using mental relaxation exercises; 11) observe and master your internal monologue; 12) plan to cope rationally and overcome bad habits and addictions (by using a Counter-Flacting method I have developed); 13) evaluate your progress and adjust your Plan of Action so that your internal thinking will support your vision, goals, and actions.

Section V introduces you to The Self-Directed Change Planner. This planner guides you through a number of steps that incorporate and integrate the principles and competencies laid out in the previous sections. Similar to the Counter-Flacting approach outlined in Competency 12b, as you respond to each step in the planner you will systematically develop a plan that you will use, on a day-to-day basis, to help you remember exactly what you plan to change and how you plan to maintain the change, including how you will identify triggers, overcome barriers, and achieve your most important goals.

Section I
Finding Your Recipe For Happiness:
Starting With The End in Mind

What is Happiness and the HAP?

In keeping with my earlier quote, "Beginning with the end in mind," it's helpful to the process here to clarify that the "end goal" of this book is to increase happiness and serenity. In other words, devoting yourself to the 13 Competencies introduced in Section IV will increase your happiness and sense of well-being. This is because it's based on what leading behavioral and social scientists agree are the most important principles and conditions that must be included in any legitimate approach to helping people better themselves, overcome troubles, improve weaknesses, and ultimately lead happier, more serene, and healthier lives.

Another saying that is also relevant here is, "If you don't know where you are going you will have a hard time getting there." This is true with happiness. If you don't know what makes you happy and what you need to think and do to be happy, you may never get there. Moreover, those who don't know their own recipe for happiness are easily mislead by society, science, the different brands of religion, their family and friends and, above all, marketers who are constantly telling us what we need to think, do, and buy to be happy. All of this is to say that the three essential steps to achieving happiness are 1) understanding what happiness is, 2) identifying your own unique recipe for happiness, and 3) consistently applying the recipe.

The scientific literature continues to grow in consensus around the idea that happiness can be measured in a way that allows us to determine who is happy, what makes them happy, and why (Cole, 2015; Cole, 2014; Seligman, 2012; Rath & Hartner, 2010; Graham, 2009; Mcmahon, 2004; Page, Wrye & Cole, 1986). Researchers, including myself (Seligman, 2012; Deiner, 200o; Page & Cole, 1992; Page & Cole, 1991; Cole, 1985) have devised theories, models and paradigms to help describe happiness and well-being (Fordyce, 2005; Wallace, 2005; Seligman, 2004; Deiner, 2000). Although many of these theories have proven useful, they are relatively inflexible in not accounting for advances in the state-of-the-art research of what happiness is and how to measure it.

In view of the limitations connected with relying on a single theory or paradigm, many researchers and self-help gurus have adopted a trans-theoretical approach to conceptualizing and updating how they think about happiness. That is, rather than relying on one theory, they choose among the most salient factors or features of prominent, well-grounded theories for a given situation. However, in doing so they can lose the benefits of the structure provided by a theoretical model. Hence, the trade-off for inflexibility is a loss of structure provided by a theoretical paradigm.

In view of this conundrum related to how to define and handle the ever growing knowledge that has been discussed at some length by my co-authors and me in the early 90s (Cole, Holtgrave & Rios, 1993), I'm introducing a psychodynamic approach here that has helped me objectively conceptualize and measure the outcomes of therapy and/or self-directed change. The principle advantage of this approach is that it combines the flexibility of a trans-theoretical approach with the structure of a paradigm. The approach I am introducing here is called the "Happiness Algorithm Planner" (HAP). In recognition of issues I mentioned above and the fact that no definition can be inclusive and acceptable to all, the HAP does not restrict you to one model of describing happiness or well-being in the process of determining the factors most relevant to accomplishing behavior change. Instead, it transforms the reliance on a single researcher's population-based correlates or causal determinants of happiness to an emphasis on the values and perceptions of each individual who uses the model to isolate his or her own unique recipe for happiness. Furthermore, the HAP helps the user draw upon the stated principles of several models (the trans-theoretical model) in an attempt to be thorough, comprehensive, and up-to-date with contemporary thinking around what constitutes true happiness.

The basic assumptions underlying the HAP model are as follows: 1) happiness is a subjective state that is based on an individual's perception, 2) individuals can reliably and honestly report their perceived state of happiness as well as increases and decreases in their status, 3) with time and the right support, individuals are capable of determining what makes them more or less happy, and 4) thinking and behaving in ways that do not increase happiness is irrational. In view of these assumptions, I define happiness as a psychological state of subjective well-being that results from thinking and living rationally—in a way that is consistent with what a person knows, via use of the HAP, makes him or her happy.

After applying the process for an extended period of time you will begin to isolate the ingredients to your personal happiness algorithms (your happiness recipe). At that point you can begin to make informed decisions about how to systematically go about increasing your happiness and sense of well-being.

The good news in all of this is that you can isolate what you are thinking or doing to cause pain, and adjust accordingly. In fact, the express purpose of the exercises related to the 13 Competencies introduced in Section IV is to help you reassert yourself in rational ways that lead to greater happiness.

To help you better understand my point, I suggest that you try experimenting with the Happiness Algorithm Planner (HAP) introduced here as a means of beginning to try to identify your own unique happiness recipe. The HAP will help you begin the process of isolating what makes you happy and then establishing a plan to systematically increase your overall happiness. In Column 1 list those dimensions of happiness that, based on your experience, make the most sense to you. To assist you with the things you might include in this column, I have provided you list factors that prominent researchers believe serve as ingredients of happiness.

Table 1
The Happiness Algorithm Planner (HAP)

*My Happiness Factors (**Each Factor Must Prove to be Rational)	What I need to think more about	What I need to think less about	What I need to do more of	What I need to do less of	Where I need to spend more time and with whom	Where I need to spend less time and with whom
Positive Emotion						
Engagement						
Positive Relationships						
Meaning						
Accomplishment						
Gratitude						
Positive Self-Image						

Decide on your own factors, or choose from among those "Happiness Ingredients" listed in Table 2.

** Rational factors are those that increase happiness. For example, if you include "Relationships" as one of your "Happiness Ingredients," and you discover that relationships don't contribute to your happiness, you can label this ingredient as "irrational" and remove it from your version of the HAP.

As you begin to use the HAP you will note that it's kind of like playing the game "Hot and Cold" where you use feedback from your experience and environment to determine what helps you get warmer (closer to happiness) and what causes you to get cooler (farther from happiness). In keeping with this analogy, an example of "getting cooler" would be evidenced by chronic psychological pain. When you experience depression or anxiety, these painful emotions are telling you that your approach to happiness is somehow deficient. Conversely, if your application of the HAP causes you to experience a discernible increase in happiness, you know that what you are thinking and doing is causing you to get "warmer."

More specifically, complete the HAP, shown here as Table 1 by: 1) listing the factors that you think contribute to your happiness in Column 1. For ideas about what researchers consider to be some of the best predictors of happiness, refer to Table 2 (Happiness Factors Based on Research Findings of Prominent Happiness and Life Satisfaction Researchers), and 2) in Columns 2-7, answer the questions that relate to each "happiness predictor" you have listed in Column 1. For example, the examples of "Happiness Ingredients" illustrated in Table 2, lists "positive emotion" as a predictor of happiness. If you agree and list positive emotion in Column 1, ask yourself 1) what do I need to think more about to increase my positive emotion, 2) what do I need to think less about to increase my positive emotion, 3) what do I need to do more of to increase my positive emotion, 4) what do I need to do less of to increase my positive emotion, 5) where do I need to spend more time and with whom to increase my positive emotion, 6) where do I need to spend less time and with whom to increase my positive emotion. Continue filling out the HAP until you have asked the six questions listed in Columns 2-7 of each of your "happiness ingredients" listed in Column 1. You will soon notice that the information you derive from this process will give you some concrete ideas that you can apply immediately in the interest of improving your quest toward finding your own tailor-made recipe for happiness.

Happiness is not to be achieved at the command of emotional whims. Happiness is not the satisfaction of whatever irrational wishes you might blindly attempt to indulge. Happiness is a state of non-contradictory joy—a joy without penalty or guilt, a joy that does not clash with any of your values and does not work for your own destruction, not the joy of escaping from your mind, but of using your mind's fullest power, not the joy of faking reality, but of achieving values that are real, not the joy of a drunkard, but of a producer. Happiness is possible only to a rational man, the man who desires nothing but rational goals, seeks nothing but rational values and finds his joy in nothing but rational actions.

- Ayn Rand, Atlas Shrugged

Table 2
Happiness Factors Based on Research Findings of Prominent Happiness and Life Satisfaction Researchers

Researcher	Happiness Ingredients
Michael W. Fordyce, "The 14 Traits of Happy People"	1) Be more active and keep busy; 2) Spend more time socializing; 3) Be productive at meaningful work; 4) Get better-organized and plan things out; 5) Stop worrying; 6) Lower your expectations and aspirations; 7) Develop positive optimistic thinking; 8) Get present-oriented; 9) WOAHP—work on a healthy personality; 10) Develop an outgoing, social personality; 11) Be yourself; 12) Eliminate the negative feelings and problems; 13) Close relationships are #1 source of happiness; 14) Happy people place a very strong value on happiness.
Martin Seligman, "Flourish: A Visionary New Understanding of Happiness and Well-being"	1) Pleasure (tasty foods, warm baths, etc.), 2) Engagement (or flow, the absorption of an enjoyed yet challenging activity), 3) Relationships (social ties have turned out to be extremely reliable indicators of happiness), 4) Meaning (a perceived quest or belonging to something bigger), and 5) Accomplishments (having realized tangible goals).
Ed Diener, "Happiness: Unlocking the Mysteries of Psychological Wealth"	1) Psychological wealth is more than money; 2) It is also your attitudes, goals, and engaging activities at work; 3) Happiness not only feels good, but is beneficial to relationships, work, and health; 4) It is helpful to set realistic expectations about happiness; 5) No one is intensely happy all of the time; and 6) Thinking is an important aspect to happiness.
Gallup-Healthways Project	Life balance is important to happiness and includes 1) how you evaluate your life, 2) physical health, 3) emotional health, 4) healthy behavior, 5) work environment, and 6) your basic access to develop and prioritize strategies to help your community thrive and grow.

Table 2
Happiness Factors Based on Research Findings of Prominent Happiness and Life Satisfaction Researchers

Researcher	Happiness Ingredients
The Seattle Area Happiness Initiative	1) Rational self-image, 2) psychological maturity and well-being, 3) physical health, 4) time or work-life balance, 5) social connection and community vitality, 6) education, 7) access to arts, culture, and recreation, 8) environmental quality and access to nature, 9) good governance, 10) material well-being, 11) meaning, 12) accomplishments, and 13) personal and interpersonal character (worth and potential, rights and responsibilities, fairness and justice, care and consideration, effort and excellence, social responsibility, and personal integrity), skills (self-control, delay of gratification, persistence, critical thinking, coping with peer pressure, conflict resolution, prioritizing competing standards, goal setting).

Inner happiness is a quality of spirit which must be earned by a victory over our weaknesses and an upward reach for the perfection of our character. It is like swimming upstream. It is found in the great efforts and achievements of life and in faithful devotion to duty. - Unknown

Once again, the end goal of this book is to help you systematically re-engineer or reprogram your beliefs, thoughts, actions, and view of yourself in a way that will help you achieve a state of happiness regardless of what is going on in your life. This is important given that those who are ignorant of their "happiness recipe" will invariably think and do things that make you unhappy without even knowing it. This said, the purpose of the resiliency competencies and change tools are to help you create a vision of your highest and best self and create a plan to realize this vision toward increasing your overall happiness and contentment in life. With time, applying the process—if my claims about the process are true, and they are—will enlarge, deepen, broaden, and amplify your highest aspirations for happiness, health, and a sense of true serenity. It will bring about a fundamental change in your beliefs, heart, and life.

Section II
Oh Say, What is Truth and,
How does it Relate to Rationality and Happiness?

The process, tools, and techniques I introduce here are based on the concept of rationality. The key criteria used to determine whether something is rational is objective truth. That is, if something is not true, it's not rational. With this in mind, I will briefly review my thoughts on both truth and rationality as a means of setting the stage for the ideas and techniques that follow.

I am always humored by the phone calls I get from potential clients asking how much I charge for a session. As I mentioned earlier, I typically ask them if their sole criteria for selecting a therapist is cost. And, in many instances, they say yes. At that point I try to explain to them that selecting a person who will sit and listen to your deepest secrets and, in turn, attempt to help you get better should take into consideration more than merely saving a few dollars. This is because not all therapists, just like not all attorneys or plumbers or pilots, etc., are the same. There is a great joke that makes my point. It goes something like this, "Do you know what they call a medical student who graduates last in his class?" The response is typically, "No, what do they call a medical student who graduates last in her class?" And, the punch line is, "They call a medical student who graduates last in his or her class, a doctor!" This analogy and example is my preface to this section of the book, which is designed to remind you that not all "self-help" or "self-directed change processes" are the same. Most are written by individuals who are effective writers but lack in experience and have very little background or understanding of behavioral science. And some are simply great story tellers who play on the existential, hedonistic leanings of humans who want to find a shortcut to paradise and greatness. This is to say that this book costs more than most self-help books because the principles and process described here are both scientifically (truth) based and clinically proven to be effective.

As was just mentioned, an essential element that serves as a defining characteristic of a rational self-identity, rational thinking, and rational living, is that they are all based on scientific truth, i.e., logical and consistent with known facts and reality. With this caveat in mind, I believe it's important to address the growing popularity of moral relativism. This irrational philosophy often competes with universal and unchanging principles that must be applied to bring about effective individual and interpersonal change, growth, and true happiness.

My concern about "moral relativism" comes out of my experiences across the world, which demonstrate the irrationality of this philosophy that simply doesn't stand up against natural laws. Rather, it's based on theoretical fun and games comprised of "made up rules" that simply don't make sense in the real world.

In short, many of the proponents of moral relativism act as if they believe the universe rearranges itself to accommodate their view of reality. This is evidenced by their attempts to either deny or attempt to re-write natural laws for expediency sake by simply justifying irrational attitudes and actions that are convenient rather than being based on collective wisdom and science. For example, a true moral relativist would not consider it a problem if a man cheated on his wife as long as his wife did not find out. On the surface and in the moment, this makes some sense. However, when the wife who is being cheated on later discovers she has HIV or an STD, the relativist's hedonistic existential argument that "if it feels good, do it" breaks down on many levels. Why? Because the irrational idea that one human being can violate the trust of another human being without consequences is based on a lie. The truth is, all actions have consequences and simply justifying an action does not remove the consequences. Put another way, those who practice the philosophy of moral relativism promote the irrational belief that we can think or do anything we want to think or do without any real predictable consequences. Once again, the truth is, we can think or do what we want to do but, in most cases, we have no control over the consequences that follow the natural laws of our universe.

For many years I worked in the area of HIV prevention, both in the US and abroad. During this time I was tirelessly trying to persuade individuals and populations about the dangers of certain behaviors. During this time I had a dream that was no doubt a projection of my frustrations related to my failure to convince many people to change their irrational behaviors. In the dream I saw a large building, and in the building were many people who were randomly running across a room in the center of the building. In the middle of the room was a huge opaque crystal about the same diameter as a large oak tree. As people ran across the room, those who went directly through the center of the room ran into the crystal. The effects were devastating. When I saw this, I went to the center of the room and started yelling out a warning about the presence of the crystal. In spite of this warning, many individuals continued to run directly into the solid mass, which began to turn red because of the trauma experienced by those who collided with the crystal while running as fast as they could. When I awoke I realized I was simply releasing some pent up frustration in my nightmare. My frustration was with the fact that those individuals I was trying to help were simply dismissing the negative consequences of their irrational actions.

For example, on one assignment to Uganda where I was working on the AIDS problem, I was staying in the only modern hotel in the capital city of Kampala. After spending the day in villages where in some cases it was estimated that 1 in 3 adults were infected with the virus that causes AIDS, I would come back to my hotel where men from all over the developed world were picking up female prostitutes who were, by that time, all infected with the virus. These men who were away from their families for extended periods of time were justifying engaging in sexual relations with complete strangers who were giving them more than transitory pleasure. In speaking with some of these individuals it was obvious that they had the irrational belief that they were immune to the consequences of their behavior. What was most disturbing was their callous disregard for how their behaviors could, and in many cases would, impact their loved ones who were ignorant of what was going on in the lives of these men.

By now I've used the word consequences many times in my attempt to explain what I mean by the effects of decisions made on the basis of irrational thoughts and actions. This is because consequences are inevitable in the application of principles that are based on truth. To argue otherwise is to say that there is no truth and no law governing the universe. It's like saying it's OK to put water in your gas tank instead of gas. After all, both water and gasoline are liquids; therefore, it does not make any difference what kind of liquid you put in a fuel tank because all liquids are created equal, right?

Other examples of how ridiculous it is to believe that there are no consequences associated with certain irrational beliefs and behaviors or that "consequences are relative" include the idea that a person can substitute rat poison for flour when baking cookies without causing harm to those who eat them, or that five different people can add the same column of numbers and get different results and that all results are correct, or that a person can drive a car from New York to Amsterdam without getting wet, or that it's OK for a dog to drink antifreeze instead of water because it tastes better. My point here is that there are countless examples of natural laws all around us, suggesting that all things in our universe must adhere to these laws.

As I explained in the preface of this book, my experiences as a therapist have shown me over and over again that universal laws also apply to human behavior. I call them universal because they apply across cultures, time periods, races, and religions.

The existence of universal laws is actually a good thing because they help us recognize that our behaviors will have consequences. Once we learn and respect these "laws," we can consistently reap the consequences associated with each law. This predictability provides us with a sense of certainty and control over our lives.

My experience growing up on a farm thought me about the "law" of the harvest. When we planted a garden, we took certain steps to ensure that we reaped the benefits of our labors: we tilled the ground, planted good seeds, fertilized, weeded, watered, and protected our crops. This universal law of farming actually applies in the world of psychology because theories that cannot replicate the consequences of universal laws of human behavior have no value. Unfortunately, sometimes theories taught to graduate students in psychology programs ignore common sense truths that are learned through experience.

I saw an example of the inadequacies of graduate clinical psychology training play out in a small rural community during our annual summer parade. While moving slowly down main street one of the small trucks pulling a float suddenly stopped running. Alongside the parade route where this incident happened was the newly hired "county psychologist." Wanting to be helpful, he ran out and helped guide a much larger truck in front of the stalled truck, to back up close enough so the larger truck could tow the smaller truck to the end of the parade route. After the lead truck was in place, the driver handed the new county psychologist a chain that he, in turn, connected to the hitch of the lead truck and then connected to the plastic grill cover of the stalled vehicle. When an elderly farmer witnessed this, he kindly approached the psychologist and suggested that the chain be attached to the frame of the stalled truck instead of the plastic grill. The psychologist was immediately convinced that the farmer knew what he was talking about and reattached the chain to the truck frame. What was most impressive to me at the time was that this learned doctor was humble enough to admit his mistake and make a change. This was a surprise to me because I was trained by some of the leading academics in my field, and I am convinced that they would have dismissed the farmer's advice and made elaborate excuses when the plastic grill of the stalled truck broke under the pressure of the tow. This is not meant to be an attack on anyone. It's just a reminder that not everything that sounds good or looks good on paper, or that is pontificated over the altars of a major university, is rational or factual. As an academic myself, I must also admit to not always seeing things clearly. After years of working with people, many of the theories of human behavior that I taught my students as a young professor simply don't hold up in a clinical setting.

All of this is to say that there are true principles that can be learned and applied in predictable ways that will increase the likelihood of individual and interpersonal development and true happiness. In fact, it's the application of these "true principles" and the logic they support that differentiates this book and the competencies and change process introduced in Section IV from a more simple-minded approach to self-improvement and change. For example, a blog post or a laymen's article about change will no doubt include information about the importance of goal setting. This is because it's no secret that change and personal improvement require direction. And, it's also no secret that the best way to chart a specific direction in life is to set a goal. What is a secret to individuals who have never had to earn their pay by helping people change is that the ability to achieve any goal requires 1) believing you are someone who can achieve the goal and 2) actually being someone who has what it takes to achieve the goal. Both of these conditions are necessary. However, neither of these conditions, believing or having what it takes to achieve a particular goal, independent of the other is sufficient to achieving a particular goal. They are only sufficient when they are taken together. In other words, you must believe, but believing alone is not enough to achieve. To achieve you must both believe and have what is required to achieve. This is because believing something is true does not make it true. It makes it possible, but not true. Something is true only when it's rational. And something is rational only when it's based on fact. In other words, only when it's based on fact is something actually true. This means if you believe you can do something that you can actually do, your belief is true. On the other hand, if you believe you can do something that you can't actually do, it's a fact that you believe in something that is not true. In keeping with this logic before you can expect to achieve any goal, you must believe you can achieve the goal and actually be able to achieve it.

Once again, this is to illustrate that simply saying something doesn't make it true. Universal, objective truth is elusive and can only be discovered through rigorous controlled trials and experiences that consistently demonstrate that some combination of variables always bring about the same outcome. That said, the competencies and exercises introduced and described in Section IV are based on truth because, if applied as prescribed, they predictably bring about desired changes and increased happiness. In large measure, the reason for this predictability is due to the fact that the process teaches the user how to learn and master techniques that ensure both rational thoughts and actions. With this in mind, it's important to understand what I mean by rational thoughts and behaviors.

In the most basic epistemology, rational thoughts and actions should be based on objective truth and logic. However, because not everyone's logic is actually logical, it helps to add some additional criteria when differentiating between rational and irrational thoughts and actions.

Generally speaking, behavioral scientists and those who use Cognitive Reappraisal Techniques in clinical settings agree on a number of factors that characterize rational thoughts. Most agree that for a thought to be rational it must be logical and consistent with known facts and reality; or in other words, it must be true. Based on these merits, it could follow that a rational thought will also produce feelings such as serenity and happiness and will result in personal growth and development. A rational thought will also help you overcome your problems and reach your goals. Conversely, if a thought you are thinking is not logical or has so evidence of truth, it is irrational. As a result, an irrational thought is destructive to yourself and others because it undermines your goals, will not help you solve your problems, and will not lead to happiness.

As is the case with rational thoughts, rational actions can be further clarified with the same type of criteria. Accordingly, rational actions are behaviors that are logical and have a basis in reality; contribute to health, personal growth, and emotional maturity; increase happiness; and help you achieve your goals. As with irrational thinking, an action that is illogical and not based on truth, does not help you overcome your problems, is destructive to yourself or others, and/or undermines your goals, is considered irrational.

Taken together, rational thoughts and actions translate into what I refer to as rational living. This means that any time you increase your rational thinking or actions, you are increasing your overall rationality. This is important because, based on everything I have observed in my clinics and population interventions and research, there is a direct correlation between increased rationality and happiness. In other words, if you increase your rational living, you will experience increased happiness. This said, because being happy is more rational than being unhappy, all thoughts and behaviors that increase life satisfaction are labeled "rational." Whereas, thoughts and actions that reduce life satisfaction are classified as "irrational," because they reduce happiness.

To sum up my explanation, when you are living rationally, you will be thinking thoughts and performing actions that "make you feel the way you want to feel," which is happy, healthy, serene—an overall feeling of well-being.

The connection between rationality and happiness will be explained and demonstrated in more detail in Section IV. However, before going through this explanation and how it relates to building resilience and increasing happiness, the next section will provide you with a deeper level of understanding regarding the principles, assumptions, and logic that must be taken into consideration when making a serious attempt at self-improvement.

Section III
Principles, Assumptions, Conditions, and Logic Models for Understanding and Psychological Resilience & Self-Improvement

As was just mentioned, I believe the principles and processes described in this book are universally true because they have worked in the past, they work now and, without exception, they will work in the future. All of this is conceptually illustrated in this book using what I have labeled the Stress Response Cycle (SRC).

The SRC model diagrammatically illustrates how Cognitive Reappraisal Techniques can be applied to the cycle in a way that helps build psychological resilience. In addition to discussing the SRC, I will also introduce two principles that are helpful in understanding this process. These are "Locus of Control" and "Rational Decision-Making." A working knowledge of these principles will help you both better understand the SRC and how to systematically apply the self-improvement ideas I introduce here across this conceptual model.

Figure 1: The Stress Response Cycle

Rational

More OK

Personal Status | Problems | **Stress (Pain)** | Coping (Thoughts) | Coping (Actions)

VISION

Less OK

Irrational

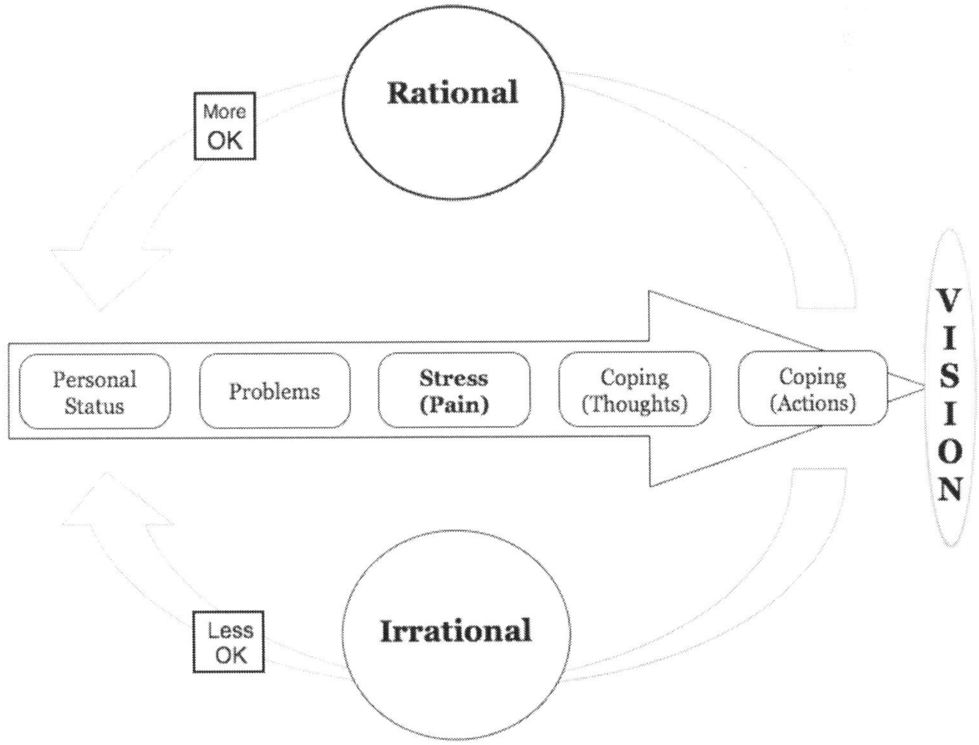

The SRC is illustrated in Figure 1. This figure diagrammatically illustrates that every hour of every day we consistently go through a process of experiencing and trying to reduce or overcome the stress caused by problems in our lives. In short, each individual has a personal status, experiences problems that result in stress, and then starts thinking and doing things that lessen or eliminate the emotional pain caused by stress. The thoughts we think and the behaviors we engage in to eliminate the pain caused by our problems are called coping decisions. These responses will make us either stronger or weaker, depending on the nature of each thought and action. I will explain the process in detail.

SRC: Personal Status

Moving from left to right across the SRC model, the first image is labeled Personal Status. This refers to how "OK" you are at any point in time. This can be measured with a rigorously valid and reliable scale that measures a number of different dimensions that make up your health and well-being. However, an easier method relies on a simple scale from 1-10, where 1 represents terrible and 10 equals excellent.

When measured on a scale from 1-10, your Personal Status represents your subjective sense of well-being. You can determine your measurement by answering three simple questions:

How are you doing on a scale from 1-10, where 1 is terrible and 10 is ideal? The answer to this question provides a general idea of your sense of well-being at a given point in time.

Why aren't you lower on the scale? The answer to this question provides insight into why you believe you are not doing worse than you could be doing. Or, put another way, the answer provides some idea concerning what is going right in your life. When I get this answer in an interview, I then say something like (assuming my client answers that the reason he or she is not lower is because he or she exercised earlier that day), "In other words, when you exercise, you feel better or your life is better. Is that correct?" This follow-up question tends to remind my clients that they can do things that make their life better.

What will it take to get higher on the scale? If the client said in response to the first question, "I'm a 7," I would ask, "What will it take to become an 8 or a 9?" Your answer to this question gives you insight into what it will take to improve your status.

There are several good reasons to keep track of how you are doing. For example, if you are typically (on most days) a 7 or an 8, and someone asks you to do something that is stressful and you, in turn, check your status and determine that you are a 3 or a 4, you will know that it's not a good idea to accept the invitation. This self-check method has saved me all kinds of problems by helping me avoid taking on more than I can handle. For instance, if my wife wanted me to take a joy ride with our five children, I would first check my Personal Status (or "OKness") before agreeing to the adventure. If I came in under 5, I would know the "joy ride" would likely turn into a "misery ride" simply because I didn't have enough in my wellness tank to tolerate all the things children do and say when they are cooped up in a car.

Another good reason for representing Personal Status on the Stress Response Cycle is to illustrate that the coping decisions you make in response to the psychological pain caused by stress inevitably impact Personal Status. This is because, in effect, Personal Status is a ratio of the number of times you cope rationally relative to the number of times you cope irrationally. If you mostly cope rationally, you are a rational person. Conversely, if you typically cope irrationally when dealing with the pain caused by the problems and stress in your life, you are an irrational person. This is in no way to say that you are a bad person. It's simply a statement of fact. Those who cope in irrational ways become irrational. This phenomenon will be clarified below.

SRC: Problems

Once again, moving from left to right, the second image on the SRC is labeled Problems, which, in this context, represent those people, places, and things that you encounter on a daily basis that cause stress. They come in all sizes, from small to very large.

From a psychological perspective, problems are those things we register in our minds as discrepancies between the way things are and the way we would like them to be. In a broad sense, a problem exists when an individual becomes aware of a significant difference between what actually is and what is desired. For example, if you wake up with a pain in your shoulder and you do not want to experience pain (only the true masochist does), you have a problem—you are experiencing physical pain. If the undesirable pain is severe, the discrepancy between your desire to be like most people—pain free—is large. Therefore, you have a big problem, which will cause stress and motivate you to make coping decisions.

Based on my clinical experience, psychological discrepancies that people label or perceive to be "problems" are different for each person. That is, what is perceived to be a problem for one individual may be quite different from what is considered problematic to that person's spouse, friend, child, or the person next door. For example, some people love to get attention in public settings whiles others are terrified. Some people love to exercise while others hate to sweat. Some people desire great wealth while others are satisfied with small means. Some parents expect perfection from their children while others are happy if their children don't go to jail.

SRC: Stress

As with problems, humans experience stress from birth. Stress, whether it's acute, episodic, or chronic, is a normal response to anything that makes us feel keyed up, threatened, or upset (Cole, 2015; Cole, 2014; Cole, 2013; Cole, Tucker & Friedman, 1986; Cole, 1985). This is why, when a person experiences a problem, he or she also experiences stress. In other words, when people, places, or things are not the way we want them to be, we experience stress, which is in many cases painful.

Stress can be a good thing when it motivates you to escape from a dangerous situation or when it helps you stay energetic and alert. However, when it causes chronic psychological or physical pain, it's a message to your brain that something is wrong.

Because almost nothing focuses the mind like pain, when problem-induced stress (whether physical or psychological or both) is detected and, especially when it becomes intolerable, individuals experience urges, impulses, and temptations to begin thinking and doing things to reduce or eliminate the pain. These thoughts and actions are called coping decisions.

SRC: Coping Thoughts

The thoughts you think to eliminate problem-induced stress and pain are called Coping Thoughts. These thoughts can be labeled as rational or irrational, depending on whether or not they legitimately improve your personal status and well-being.

More specifically, for a coping thought to be rational it must be logical and based on truth, produce feelings of serenity and happiness, and help you solve your problems and reach your goals. Moreover, rational coping thoughts help develop and sustain a rational self-identity that leads to a sense of well-being.

Conversely, if a thought you are thinking is not logical or true, it is not a rational coping thought and therefore will not help you feel the way you want to feel (i.e., you will still experience overwhelming feelings of stress), nor will it help you overcome your problems or reach your goals.

SRC: Coping Actions

Rational coping thoughts tend to result in rational coping actions. Just as is the case with coping thoughts, Coping Actions can be classified as either rational or irrational. Similar to rational coping thoughts, rational coping actions can be further clarified with similar criteria. Accordingly, rational coping actions are logical, based on truth, contribute to health and happiness, and help you overcome your problems and reach your goals.

As with irrational coping thoughts, irrational coping actions are not logical or based on truth, do not help you feel the way you want to feel (healthy, happy, serene, etc.), do not help you overcome your problems, and/or undermine your goals. These irrational thoughts are destructive to you and others; they do not help you cope with stress in a healthy way. Furthermore, irrational coping actions are like shortcuts to overcoming pain. Those who prefer these "quick fixes" to stress—like drinking to relax, or smoking marijuana to forget, or quitting a job to escape an uncomfortable workplace, or retreating from a stressful situation, like giving a public presentation—tend to become emotionally weaker over time. In fact, the worst thing we can possibly do when we have an anxiety disorder is to "retreat from people, places, and things" that make us anxious. This is because although the retreat relieves the stress caused by the anxiety-provoking situation, at the same time it reinforces the irrational behavior we are trying to overcome—the tendency to retreat from things that make us anxious.

Locus of Control and Rational Decision-Making

Figure 2 illustrates how, when taken together, coping thoughts and actions represent a point of decision or "Decision Point." To clearly understand this idea it's helpful to understand the concepts of locus of control and self-regulation and how these concepts impact our decisions around coping.

In 1954, a personality psychologist, Julian B. Rotter, promoted a concept called locus of control. This construct refers to the extent to which individuals believe they can control events affecting them. The word "locus" (Latin for "location" or "place") is conceptualized as either external locus of control_(meaning individuals believe their decisions and life are controlled by chance or fate) or internal locus of control (individuals believe they can control their life and how they respond to people, places, and things that are outside their control). Individuals with a mostly external locus of control tend to blame things outside their control (the actions of other people or events in their environment) on how they think and decide to behave. For example, when these individuals get a poor rating at work, they tend to blame their work environment or work colleagues or their manager for the negative rating. Conversely, those who have mostly internal locus of control tend to focus on how they, themselves, decide to react to these external influences. When these individuals get poor ratings at work they take responsibility for the poor ratings by attributing the rating to their ineffective or limited abilities rather than to their environment.

Figure 2: The SRC Decision Point

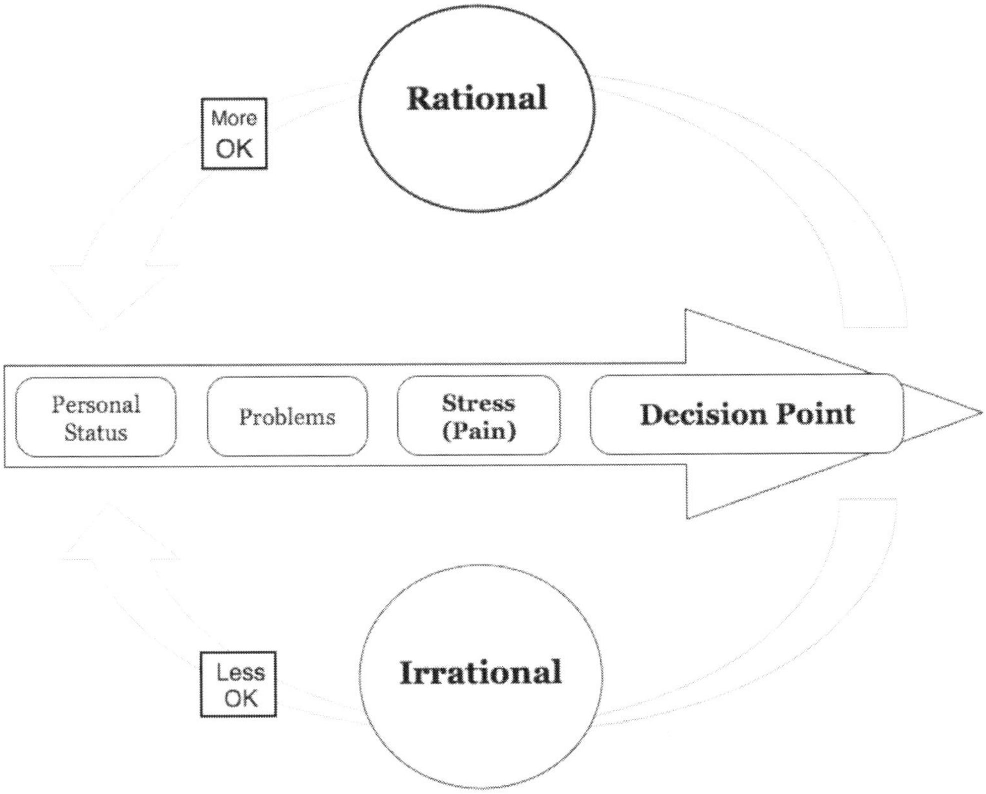

Because individuals with mostly internal locus of control take responsibility for their failures and their successes, they feel empowered. This is evidenced by studies demonstrating that these individuals have better academic achievement, better interpersonal relations, greater efforts to learn, positive attitudes to exercise, less cigarette smoking, less hypertension, fewer heart attacks. On the other hand, those who assign responsibility for their problems and their progress to forces outside their control tend to feel like victims and feel powerless. Studies have shown that these individuals are more resigned to conditions "as they are," exhibit less drive to promote their health or to deal with health issues, and have lower levels of psychological adjustment.

The Stress Response Cycle illustrates how locus of control plays out and impacts our personal well-being. That is, at the Decision Point (see Figure 2), we repeatedly make coping decisions about whether or not to respond (cope) rationally or irrationally when challenged by our problems. If we have mostly internal locus of control, we are more likely to accept and believe that the energy required to think and act rationally will be efficacious and result in benefits to our overall well-being. If, on the other hand, at the point of decision we do not believe our thoughts or actions will have any impact on or improve our overall well-being, we will be less inclined to think and act rationally. This is especially true given that, over the short-term, it is much harder to think and act rationally than it is to think and act irrationally. This is because, in the here and now, the "irrational path" or "the path of least resistance" or the "softer, easier way" is much easier to follow. This is largely due to the fact that almost nothing focuses the mind like pain. Because of this, humans are anxious to relieve the pain as soon as possible—especially when it's severe. This tendency to want rapid pain relief tempts us to look for "quick fixes," which can give immediate relief, but over the long-term, these "quick fixes" can result in even more pain.

An experience with a past client with chronic pain provides a valuable example. This client fell off a ladder and damaged his spinal nerves, causing debilitating pain, radiculopathy, and degenerative disc disease. To help my patient deal with the pain, his physician prescribed increasingly larger does of opiate medications. This "quick fix," which didn't really fix anything but simply masked the problem, resulted in long-term opiate use. This, in turn, resulted in mental impairment, reduction of physical balance, elimination of sex drive, memory loss, depression, suicidal thoughts, and suppression of the pituitary gland and hypothalamus, which causes non-production of testosterone and endocrinological problems. In other words, the thing that seemed to be most rational because it gave some relief (opiate use) actually became the larger problem, which my client spent several months trying to fix, without success, until he came to me and applied the Counter-Flacting Process (which I will describe in Competency 12b). As an update, he is now completely drug free and managing his pain using hypnotherapy and the other methods that you will find in this book.

Some other examples of irrational thoughts and actions, which qualify as "quick fixes," and their corresponding rational thoughts and actions are illustrated in Table 3 . As you can see, what is listed in Column 1 requires very little thought or effort, while those things in Column 2 require both. Those who have high external locus of control (have very little faith that they can control their thoughts and actions and, if they do, these efforts will not make a difference in the long run) are much more likely to opt for "The Path of Least Resistance" than those individuals who have an internal locus of control; they typically believe their rational thoughts and efforts will make a difference if not in the short-term, then definitely over the long-term.

Table 3
Comparison of Irrational Thoughts & Actions Against Rational Thoughts & Actions

Irrational Thoughts & Actions "The Path of Least Resistance"	Rational Thoughts & Actions "The More Difficult Path"
Not setting goals	Setting goals
Not doing what is required to achieve goals	Doing what is required to achieve goals
Remaining sedentary when feeling emotional stress	Exercising
Screaming and raging when feeling angry	Staying calm when experiencing feelings of anger
Getting drunk to ease the pain of divorce or abandonment	Talking to a therapist when experiencing the pain of divorce or abandonment
Playing the lottery in an attempt to get rich	Getting an advanced degree and excelling in a professional field, or starting and excelling in a business

The material provided in the next table (Table 4) further illustrates the benefits of doing what is required to adopt a sense of internal locus of control and, in turn, investing the time and effort required to decide to think and act rationally. Similar to the last table, both columns in the next table illustrate decisions that you can make that can be classified as either rational or irrational. Specifically, Column 1 illustrates irrational decisions and Column 2 illustrates more rational ones.

Hopefully, you recognize the truth that you can consistently decide to think and act rationally and that, over the long run, this decision will make you a happier, healthier, more resilient, and more effective person. This decision also requires you to abandon the "victim mentality" of the external locus of control perspective and adopt the empowered mentality of the internal locus of control perspective, which puts you clearly in charge of your life and how you interpret and react to what happens to you. As with everything else included in this table, this rational approach to living requires consistently making rational decisions. And, according to the famous motivational speaker Tony Robbins, "It is in your moments of decision that your destiny is shaped." Frankly, based on what I have observed in working with individuals for many decades, the decisions you make dictate the life you lead and will ultimately determine whether or not you enjoy your life and consider yourself to be a success or a failure.

Table 4
Comparison of Characteristics and Consequences of Irrational and Rational Decisions

Irrational Decisions (They typically make me weaker.)	Rational Decisions (They help me become stronger.)
Decide to think and act irrationally—in a way that undermines my goals.	Decide to think and act rationally—in a way that is consistent with my goals.
When I fail at something, I can decide to give up.	When I experience failure, I can decide to do what it takes to determine what went wrong and what I need to do to succeed the next time.
Decide to get wasted when I am upset about a problem.	Decide to use a proven problem-solving approach when I am upset about a problem.
Decide to be pessimistic.	Decide to be optimistic.
Decide to regret the past.	Decide to learn from the past.
Decide to worry about the future.	Decide to prepare for the future.
Decide to neglect my health and experience preventable health conditions.	Decide to live a healthy, balanced life.
Decide to not do what it takes to prepare for a career.	Decide to go to trade school or college and become prepared for a good job.
Decide not to network or send out resumes.	Decide to develop and send out an impressive resume and network.

Table 4
Comparison of Characteristics and Consequences of Irrational and Rational Decisions

Irrational Decisions (They typically make me weaker.)	Rational Decisions (They help me become stronger.)
Decide to get a divorce.	Decide to go to marriage counseling.
Decide to hit and yell and scream at my kids when they disobey me.	Decide to read parenting books and learn how to effectively teach and discipline my children.
Decide to be reactive.	Decide to be proactive.
Decide to hold a grudge.	Decide to forgive.
Decide to think thoughts that make me sad or anxious.	Decide to think thoughts that make me happy and calm.
Decide to focus on what I don't have in life.	Decide to count my blessings.
Decide to surrender to the negative energy of others.	Decide to take positive energy (enthusiasm) with me wherever I go.
Decide to see problems as setbacks.	Decide to see problems as opportunities.

Resilience Development Cycle (RDC)

The importance of psychological resilience is captured in a quote credited to Ardomore Herophiles who, in 30 BC, was reported to have said "When Health is absent, Wisdom cannot reveal itself; Art cannot become manifest; Strength cannot be exerted; Wealth is useless and reason is powerless." As will be discussed in some detail, health and personal resilience are essential to happiness and well-being.

Personal psychological resilience has to do with our ability to cope with and bounce back from the stress-inducing problems and adversity that we encounter on a day to day basis. High levels of psychological resilience (or mental toughness) increase an individual's ability to cope with and recover from high levels of adversity and stress. Whereas, low levels of psychological resilience means you will have a limited ability to endure and rebound in response to the challenges of life and the distress that follows.

Resilience is not developed in times of great stress. Rather, it is what we rely upon to retain our rationality when we are challenged with any size problem. In other words, it's too late to obtain resilience when you are in the midst of a crisis. Either you will have developed the resilience you need to ride out the crisis, or not. If you don't have it and you face severe challenges, your ability to cope rationally will be severely limited.

Because humans have needs across a number different dimensions (e.g., mental, emotional, physical, social and spiritual), personal resilience can be impacted by anything that impacts one dimension in either a positive or negative way. In other words, if you exercise on a regular basis (Tucker, Cole & Friedman, 1986), your resilience across all dimensions will, in most cases, be impacted in a positive way. Similarly, if you don't learn the skills or take the time to develop meaningful friendships and social support, your resilience will be impacted negatively given that you will have no one to turn to when you have exhausted all of your personal resources.

The logic model that I use to illustrate how you can build personal resilience is called the Resilience Development Cycle (RDC). The RDC is similar to the SRC (Stress Response Cycle) in that it illustrates how our personal decisions impact our well-being or, in this case, our personal resilience. The concept illustrated by this model is important to the process of self-directed change because it explains why some people are more tolerant of stress than others. It also illustrates how the choices we make about how we use our discretionary time make us weaker or stronger.

The RDC is provided here as Figure 3. This figure shows that, at its most basic level, human resilience is impacted by how we choose to use our discretionary time.

Figure 3: Resiliency Development Cycle

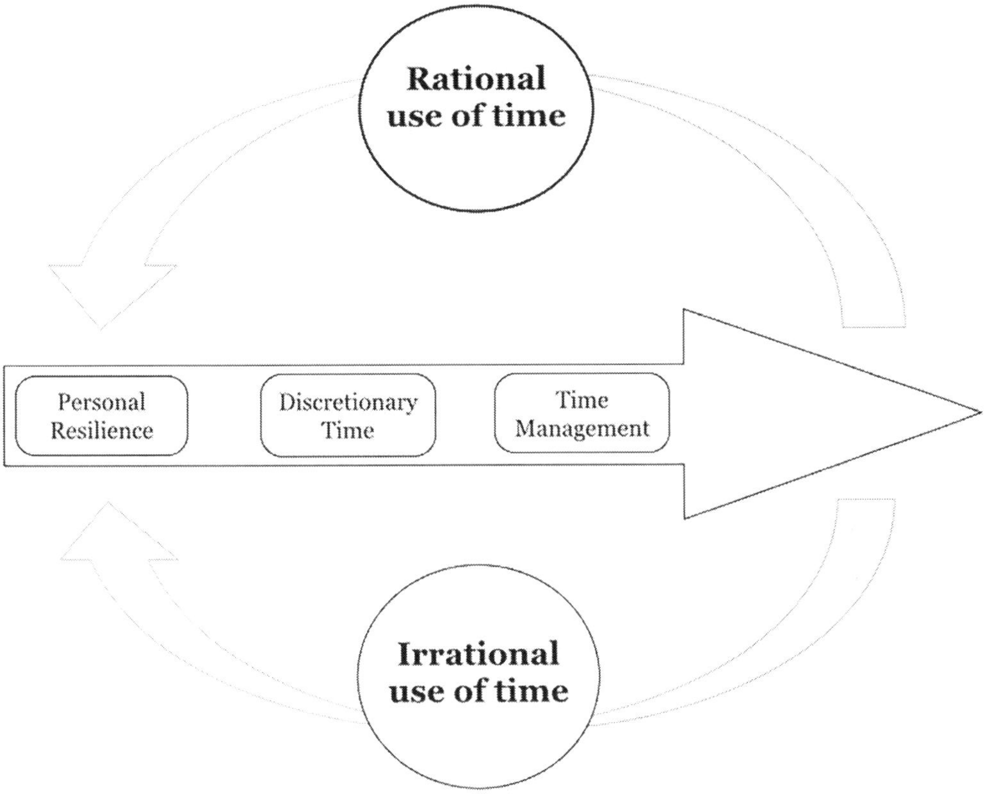

Starting from the left hand side of Figure 3 and moving to the right, the assumption is that everyone has a finite amount of resilience at any given point in time. The model also assumes that each one of us has a certain amount of discretionary time. And finally, the model assumes correctly that each one of us has the ability to manage our discretionary time in either rational or irrational ways. And, in the case of this model, the rational use of discretionary time means the choice to use this time in a way that makes a person more resilient instead of less resilient. For example, if an unemployed person who says he or she wants to get a job lounges around watching TV most of the day, this would be considered irrational given that watching TV instead of building a good resume, searching reputable web sites for online job listings, making phone calls, visiting employment centers and/or exercising to remain fit, is an irrational way of using discretionary time because it does not help the person become more resilient in the area of employment.

This is all to say that personal resilience is important because it is the energy reserve we have to prepare for life's inevitable difficulties, recover from setbacks, deal with problems, and consciously choose to cope in rational ways in response to any amount of stress induced pain. It's the fuel we need to become better instead of bitter in the face of hardship. The fact is, human beings have known for millennia that if we don't develop resilience and wisely prepare for the future, we will struggle. This is exemplified in a Proverb in the Old Testament of The Bible, as follows (Proverbs 6: 6-11, New American Standard Bible):

6Go to the ant, O sluggard,
    Observe her ways and be wise,
7Which, having no chief,
    Officer or ruler,
8Prepares her food in the summer
    And gathers her provision in the harvest.
9How long will you lie down, O sluggard?
    When will you arise from your sleep?
10A little sleep, a little slumber,
    A little folding of the hands to rest"—
11Your poverty will come in like a vagabond
    And your need like an armed man.

Building resilience is like the time you put into studying for a test. If it's a very simple test, you don't need to study very much. If it's a big test, you should study a lot and not wait until the last night before the test to start studying.

Just as it takes time to prepare for a big test, it takes time to build psychological resilience. With this in mind, the 13 Competencies introduced and explained in Section IV provide guidance on how to develop a balanced approach to building and sustaining personal resilience over time.

The "Path of Least Resistance" and "Self-Sabotage" Battle the "Why" of Change

I have one more caveat that needs to be explained before introducing the 13 Competencies. This has to do with an important principle that is at the heart of the mystery of why people, with the best intentions to make personal changes or to recover from serious addiction, tend to sabotage their best intentions and fail. The key to this mystery is unveiled in a simple diagram in Figure 4, which is an attempt to illustrate the battle between the old and new ways of thinking and doing things—your old self and your new self.

Figure 4:
Tug of War Between Why You Should Versus
Why You Should Not Change

The fact is, whenever we set out to change we immediately encounter resistance. A simple example of this is in dieting. You may have said to yourself after a big meal that you will never eat that much again. And, in most cases you don't until the next time you are offered a large, tasty meal. A simple explanation of this is that people give in to the pain of hunger because of a lack of self-discipline. Although this is part of the reason, it ignores the real reason. The reason people who vow to quit overeating and fail is because they don't have an important enough goal to carry them past their hunger pains. I call this goal the "Why" of change. This is because whenever we are stressed, we always resort to "The Path of Least Resistance" unless we have a good reason not to.

"The Path of Least Resistance" or the "easier, softer way" is a powerful force that keeps us from growing. It's the reason most people don't set goals, and the reason why most people who do set them don't reach them. It's the reason an abusive person who is contrite after hurting someone goes back to the same behavior the next time he or she is stressed. The fact is, it's easier to do nothing than it is to do something, easier not to try than it is to try, easier to focus on yourself than it is on others, easier to go along with the crowd that it is to adopt a dissenting opinion, easier to settle for a "quick fix" than it is to patiently do what it takes to get the results you want, and easier not to entertain random thoughts than it is to control your thinking. The favorite internal mantra of those who live on this path is simple, "If it feels good do, and do it until it hurts."

As I alluded to above, the only way to overcome the gravitational pull of the least resistant path is to set a goal that has a stronger gravitational pull. This is because the strongest pull always wins.

Setting a goal that can overcome the easy path is not that simple. In fact, the recipe for doing this is one of the resilience competencies (Competency 6) discussed in Section IV. What I will say at this point is that it is both necessary and essential to change. Without the "big reason" to change you simply can't do it for any length of time.

Behavioral scientists have speculated that part of the reason for the tug of war between easy ways of doing things and ways that require energy and commitment has to do with the part of the brain that is programmed to keep us safe and secure. By definition, this part of the brain (the cerebellum and the brain-stem where reflex responses arise, repetitive routines are stored, and where fight or flight attributes are remembered) is more emotional and reflexive than the executive functioning parts of the brain (the cerebrum, frontal lobes, and cortex, where logic, conscious thought, empathy, and art are created) and is considered to be biased against change and to prefer stability.

Given that there is a part of our brain that is pulling against change, it makes sense that in order to change, we must somehow overcome the cerebellum's emotional concerns about the unstable condition induced by making life changes. This is to say, this reflexive part of the brain works against even those life changes that are in our best interest simply because they create a sense of uncertainty. This means that the psychology of change must take into consideration the part of the brain that has concerns about any type of change or instability. Consequently, to be effective, the process of change must persuade the part of us worried about any instability that change is good and in our best interest. The process described in Section IV does just that. And, it does it in a way that convinces the cerebellum and the cerebrum to work together in bringing about the desired change.

Magical Thinking is Not Magical, or Effective

Another form of self-sabotage is called Magical Thinking. This label should not be confused with "associative thinking," which is a common feature of practitioners of magic. Rather, it's a twisted way of thinking that tends to ignore the steps required to get from point A to Z.

Albert Einstein said, "Genius is 1% talent and 99% percent hard work." I have seen this play out again and again in my clinics where I have tried to help gifted and talented individuals who have successfully made a complete mess out of their lives turn their lives around and get back on a path to sanity.

Most recently, I have experienced a rash of parents making appointments for and accompanying their adult "children" to my office for help. The predominant concern is that their "child" is stuck and not making progress. When I hear this I ask the adult child (typically young men, ages 18 to early 30s) if any of his or her parent's concerns are true. In response, he or she will often say something like, "I just don't have a passion," or "I just don't have any motivation." And, in many cases, those who do have passion are unwilling to do anything until they see an opportunity to jump from where they are in space and time to a place of prominence without taking any steps in between.

One of these young men was 34 years old and was anxiously pursuing a career in Hollywood. He had great passion but was unwilling to go to film school or work for a studio because he perceived that he could "make it big" on his own. This worked for him until one day his parents stopped sending money to help him pay for his car, buy gas, pay rent, and pay for his gym membership. His elderly parents wanted to support his passion, but finally realized their son was engaging in Magical Thinking.

Although it's been around forever, it seems like Magical Thinking is becoming more popular than ever before. This may be in some part due to a popular cliché used by some contemporary self-help gurus who promise success to all those who will just "put it out there," whatever that means. Simply put, Magical Thinking involves thinking and doing things that are believed to have an impact on a specific goal, when in fact the things a person is thinking and doing actually reduce the likelihood of achieving the goal.

In keeping with the above example, the longer the young man puts off going to film school or starting to work his way up the pecking order in the film business, the less likely he is to actually succeed in the business. Even though he "thinks" he is making progress and has made up elaborate stories to convince his parents and himself that he is making progress, he is actually getting further and further behind as compared to those his age who paid the price of going to film school and working their way up the ranks. Fortunately, and to his parents' great surprise and delight, I was able to work with this young man until he put together a realistic plan that led him to take the necessary steps required to get his career on track.

Frankly, anyone who believes in Magical Thinking will struggle with what is laid out in this book, because that person will see the process involved as being "too difficult." I would ask this person, "Why does everything have to be so easy?" Having personally come out of very humble circumstances and risen to a level of success that I never would have imagined as a young man working on a ranch in Southwest, Kansas, I have come to know first-hand the truth of this popular quote by Calvin Coolidge: "Nothing in this world can take the place of persistence. Talent will not; nothing is more common than unsuccessful people with talent. Genius will not; unrewarded genius is almost a proverb. Education will not; the world is full of educated derelicts. Persistence and determination alone are omnipotent. The slogan 'press on' has solved and always will solve the problems of the human race." And I might add, Magical Thinking is often at the core of the belief system of those who think they can succeed without persistence and determination.

Finally, I think the definition of insanity is perhaps the best test as to whether or not you or one of your loved ones is engaging in Magical Thinking. That is, "If you keep doing the same thing while expecting a different outcome, you are insane." To get a different outcome, you must think and do things differently. That is, you must abandon Magical Thinking and develop goals and a plan that has been proven to get you where you want to go. This is because you can't do certain things unless you become the kind of person who does those kinds of things. This means you must study, in great detail, the lives of those who have successfully done the things you want to do, and then you must do those things with a vengeance until you achieve your desired goal.

The fact is, there are no short cuts to greatness. This was documented in the book, titled Creativity: Flow and the Psychology of Discovery and Invention, by Mihály Csíkszentmihályi. Based on hundreds of interviews with exceptional people, including business leaders, politicians, biologists and physicists, he found that those who reach great heights in life first master the fundamentals of their chosen profession. That is, none of them engaged in Magical Thinking, and all of them paid the price of success by carefully cultivating the skills, discipline, and persistence required to excel in making great contributions.

All said, one purpose of this book is to demonstrate what is actually required to achieve and sustain success, happiness, and a sense of well-being. Even if you have incorporated some Magical Thinking into your personal plans for success and life satisfaction (Who hasn't at some point in their lives?), I recommend that you read this book just to make sure you aren't missing something in your personal recipe for living.

The Psychology of Change: Assumptions, Principles, and Conditions

Have you ever wondered why most people who commit to making changes end up giving up on their goals? Part of the secret to this mystery is in the Henry Louis Menken quote that I mentioned in the introduction of this book: "There is always a well-known solution to every human problem—neat, plausible, and wrong." It's true; lasting change and personal improvement is not easy. At the same time, if done correctly, it's not hard. It simply requires following the right steps in the right sequence for the right amount of time. Taken together, the 13 Competencies presented in Section IV will provide you with the essential ingredients required to improve yourself and your relationships. These ideas are not simply theoretical fun and games. Rather, they are based on what leading behavioral and social scientists agree are the most important principles and conditions that must be addressed in an effective self-directed psychological change process (Seligman, 2012; Fordyce, 2005; Deiner, 2000; Fishbein, Bandura, Triandis, Kaufer & Becker, 1991; Page, Wrye & Cole, 1986; Cole, Friedman & Bagwell, 1986; Page & Cole, 1985; Cole, 1985; Skinner, 1953).

Specifically, to successfully set and achieve goals that lead to sustained happiness and serenity (or well-being):

- you must view yourself in rational ways. This means you must understand that the way you think about yourself (i.e., your perception of self) either increases or diminishes your state of happiness and serenity (or well-being). For example, perceiving yourself in a way that increases your happiness is a Rational Self Perception or RSP.

- you must learn to think rationally—in ways that are congruent with rational goals and a RSP;

- you must learn to act rationally—in ways that are consistent with rational goals and a RSP;

- you must have a rational plan for change—a realistic plan that works;

- you must have an internal locus of control—a belief that in the case of happiness and emotional well-being, it's not what happens to you, or your circumstances, but what you decide to think and do about what happens to you and your circumstances that counts. Those who think and behave in ways that are consistent with this assumption have internal locus of control. Whereas, those who think that they are controlled by what happens to them and/or their circumstances, have an external locus of control.

- you must form a strong positive intention (or make a commitment) to change;

- you must understand what can be done to build personal resiliency and cope in healthy, rational ways;

- you must have basic skills, including such skills as mental imagery and rehearsal, goal setting, resiliency development, coping, cognitive restructuring, critical thinking, self-discipline, delayed gratification, persistence, planning, and problem solving;

- you must master monitoring personal status and internal monologues;

- you must have the mental discipline to align your thoughts with your goals. This assumes you understand that your conscious mind has a voice. This is evident because as humans we talk to ourselves inside all of the time—i.e., we think. It's how you know what you are thinking and feeling that matters. The goal is to talk to yourself (think) in rational ways. Although it's true that we tend to become what we think about most of the time, successfully achieving a goal requires more than positive thinking. It's an oversimplification of reality. In other words, positive thinking is an additive to rational thinking; it's necessary, but not sufficient. Negative, self-critical thinking (irrational thinking) erodes confidence and obstructs success. It is irrational to think about yourself in negative, critical ways.

- you must believe (have confidence) you can do what is required to change. This is called self-efficacy.

- you must understand intrinsic and extrinsic motivation and how they impact goal-oriented thinking and action;

- you should have a positive reinforcement for doing what you plan to do;

- you should understand how to identify and overcome triggers, barriers, and self-sabotage;

- you should believe that the advantages of doing what you plan to do outweigh the disadvantages;

- you should perceive that there is more social pressure to do what you recommend than not to do it;

- you should believe what you plan to do is consistent with your self-image and does not violate your personal standards;

- you should understand that everyone who has a healthy brain can learn to live rationally;

- you should understand that rational living increases happiness and serenity—emotional well-being;

- you should understand that the brain's ability to change shape over time (Neuroplasticity) allows for changes in the brain that result from conscious changes in thinking. This means you can use your mind to change your brain for the better.

- you should understand that setting and striving toward specific goals will give you the sense that life has purpose and meaning. Furthermore, achieving goals will give you a discernible sense of accomplishment that is often referred to as success—the progressive realization of a worthy ideal. Because setting and achieving goals give you a sense of purpose and feelings of success, it's rational to set and achieve goals. Conversely, not setting goals or setting goals that you don't achieve is irrational. To be rational, a goal must specific, measurable, realistic, stated in terms of a specific time period, and you must believe you can achieve the goal (have self-efficacy or confidence) and actually be able to achieve it (have the required knowledge, skills, and abilities). This is because 1) it's irrational to assume you can achieve a goal that you don't believe you can achieve, and 2) you must become the kind of person who does the kind of thing you plan to do. You must learn to behave rationally—in ways that are consistent with rational goals and a rational self-image.

Once again, the resiliency competencies are based on these assumptions and principles. Without these assumptions, this process is just another person's attempt at passing along some "good advice."

Section IV
Resiliency Competencies for Personal Development and Recovery

As a professional who spends most of my time trying to help others, a constant concern that I share with other helping professionals can be summed up by the quotes I referenced earlier. Albert Einstein said, "Make everything as simple as possible, but not simpler," and Henry Louis Menken said, "There is always a well-known solution to every human problem—neat, plausible, and wrong." My concern is that I will provide those I am trying to help with either too much or too little information. With this in mind, I have carefully identified 13 Resiliency Competencies that build upon one another.

As I mentioned in Section III, psychological resilience is an individuals' capacity to cope with difficult life events and stress. High levels of resilience increase an individual's ability to cope with and bounce back from high levels of adversity and stress. In contrast, low levels of psychological resilience mean you will have a limited ability to endure and rebound in response to the challenges of life and the distress that follows.

As I mentioned in Section III, resilience is not developed in times of great stress. Rather, it is what we rely upon to retain our rationality when we are challenged with any size problem. In other words, it's too late to obtain resilience when you are in the midst of a crisis. Either you will have developed the resilience you need to ride out the crisis, or not. If you don't have it and you face severe challenges, your ability to cope rationally will be severely limited.

This section of the book has three end goals. These are to 1) introduce you to 13 of the most important psychological resilience competencies, 2) help you understand how to develop these competencies in yourself, and 3) teach you how to use these competencies to change whatever you want to change about yourself. Achieving these goals will help you live a life that is filled with happiness and a sense of serenity (or well-being). You you will acquire the ability to be OK when things in your life are not.

I will introduce and develop these 13 Competencies: 1) measure and monitor your psychological status; 2) communicate effectively; 3) rationally define and solve problems; 4) develop and implement a personal improvement plan; 5) create a Rational Personal Vision Statement; 6) set and achieve rational goals; 7) determine what will motivate you to change and grow; 8) identify and anticipate triggers and barriers to change and growth; 9) create a Plan of Action; 10) mentally program and internalize your RPVS, goals, and Plan of Action; 11) observe and master your internal monologue; 12) plan to cope rationally and overcome bad habits and addictions; and 13) evaluate your progress and adjust your Plan of Action.

To further clarify each of the 13 Competencies, I have listed them in Column 1 of Table 5, alongside a corresponding question in Column 2 that you can ask yourself to determine which areas you may need to work on to develop the competency.

In short, every competency and the implementation guidance that supports each competency is designed to help you systematically re-engineer or reprogram your beliefs, thoughts, actions, and how you view yourself in a way that will help you achieve and maintain a state of happiness and serenity under pressure. The process will enlarge, deepen, broaden, and amplify your highest aspirations for happiness, health, and a sense of true serenity. It will bring about a fundamental change in your beliefs, heart, and life.

Finally, if for some reason this recipe for change does not work for you, please consider following the advice given in a television commercial used to promote psychiatric services in the Southwest United States: "If you don't get help here, get it somewhere else." This is because if you don't follow some program or process that leads to more rational living, you will be like the lead character in the movie, Groundhog Day (1993). In this movie a weatherman (played by Bill Murray) finds himself living the same day over and over again until he gets it right. Truly, as I have explained before, the best definition of insanity is "thinking and doing the same thing over and over again, expecting a different outcome." With that said, I will end this introduction to the resiliency competencies by referring to one of my favorite quotes by Robert Louis Stevenson: "No man can run away from weakness. He must either fight it out or perish. And if that be so… why not now, and where you stand."

One final caveat to consider before you review the competencies is the fact that the tables provided throughout the book should be considered as guides for recording your ideas. Although there is some space to document your thinking here, I suggest in Competency 1 that you purchase a journal and simply use the tables and other spaces for writing provided in the book here as examples. You can transfer your responses to your journal and, in turn, tailor to your own liking and needs.

Table 5
Psychological Resilience Competencies and Competency Questions

Competency	Competency Questions
Measure and monitor your psychological status.	Do you routinely discern the state of your personal well-being (mindfulness)?
Communicate effectively.	Do you know how to effectively start, continue, and end a conversation?

Table 5
Psychological Resilience Competencies and Competency Questions

Competency	Competency Questions
Rationally define and solve problems.	Can you effectively conceptualize and solve problems?
Develop and implement a personal improvement plan.	Do you have a personal improvement plan? Do you consistently do what is outlined in your
Create a Rational Personal Vision Statement (RPVS).	Do you have a rational self-image?
Set and achieve rational goals.	Do you know how to effectively set and reach
Determine what will motivate you to change and grow.	Do you know how to motivate yourself to change and improve?
Identify and anticipate Triggers and Barriers to change and growth.	Can you identify and anticipate triggers and barriers that impede your personal growth and
Create a Plan of Action.	Do you know how to develop and implement a personal plan of action?
Mentally program and internalize your RPVS, goals, and Plan of	Do you know how to use mental relaxation exercises and strategies to internalize your vision
Observe and master your internal monologue.	Do you consciously observe and discipline your thoughts?
Plan to cope rationally and over-	Do you cope rationally?
Evaluate your progress and adjust your Plan of Action.	Can you evaluate your daily progress and make the necessary adjustments to ensure success?

Competency 1
Measure and Monitor Your Psychological Status

Competency 1 will help you better understand the value of keeping a daily record in the form of a journal, diary, log, or notebook. Journaling or keeping letters or diaries are ancient traditions dating back to the beginning of recorded history. This is evident in an ancient Chinese Proverb, which says, "The palest ink is better than the sharpest memory." We are more likely to accurately remember things we think and do, or plan to do, when we write them down.

In recent history, journaling has been found to result in both physical and psychological health benefits in both non-clinical and clinical populations. Because of this finding, when I begin working with a new client I often explain that one of the easiest to learn, least expensive, and most profound forms of therapy available is journaling. I explain that fully understanding any experience requires perspective that can be derived from reading your personal history over a period of days and months rather than hours or moments in time. And, that a life recorded page-by-page, day-by-day, month-by-month, and year-by-year reveals patterns, purposes, and relationships between what we think and do and what happens to us over time. When patterns do emerge, you can see more clearly the negative effects of irrational living as well as the benefits of rational thoughts and actions in a way that may have escaped you in the throng of circumstances.

Over the years my clients have used journaling as a tool for self-knowledge, self-insight, self-exploration, self-expression, self-evaluation, and self-improvement. When I have asked them to report back to me the benefits of journaling, I have received many different answers. For example, different clients have told me (I am paraphrasing) that journaling has helped them cope with traumatic experiences; entertain themselves; reframe their negative experiences into more positive experiences; achieve new perspective; ease a sense of loneliness; observe and clarify thinking; improve intuition and creativity; validate the benefits of taking certain actions; process their innermost thoughts; prevent them from making the same mistake twice; become better organized; relive joyful events; increase gratitude for things that have gone right; remind them of what it takes to come back after defeat; remain or become more focused; communicate with themselves; record their deepest concerns and thoughts, achievements, and failures; process events; "organize" their thoughts and feelings; get to know themselves better; realize and release the intensity of their anger, sadness, and other painful emotions; improve congruency between goals, thoughts, actions and their self-image; stay in the present; track patterns, trends, and improvement and growth over time; ask themselves and answer important questions; record and remember important events; brainstorm solutions to seemingly unsolvable problems and solve their problems more effectively; write about and eventually resolve disagreements with others instead of ruminating over them; record goals and promises to themselves; capture their life story for posterity; hold themselves accountable; evaluate their progress; and restore a sense of optimism, anticipation, and excitement about their goals or aspirations.

Although there are many documented benefits to journaling, the primary reason for using this technique in helping you build this competency is to teach you how to become more observant, i.e. mindful. By definition, to be rational you must be observant of what you are thinking and doing. You must also observe how your thoughts and actions contribute to, or take away from, your goals and your sense of well-being. In short, developing a habit of journaling will help you develop the habit of being observant in ways that help you extract the lessons from your experiences. For example, instead of focusing on the negative aspect of your experiences, you can pay attention to the good that comes out of things that may initially appear to be very negative.

Observing your status will help you record new insights and lessons you learn as you try new ways of thinking and living. As you review this information over time, you will gain the insights you need to break the pattern of doing the same thing and expecting a different outcome. Armed with these insights you can do what is necessary to avoid repeating the same mistakes.

Journaling will help you see your progress over time, which can motivate you to keep moving forward during difficult times. As you look back you will also notice that, in many instances, things you thought were big problems in the past might seem small today. This type of information can also serve as a "reality check" that can remind you of the fact that a vast majority of what humans worry about never happen as is so keenly observed in a quote by Mark Twain: "My life has been filled with calamities, some of which actually happened." This is consistent with a study conducted by professors as the University of Cincinnati who found that eight-five percent (yes - 85%) of what we worry about never happens. The study also reported that 79% of us handle the 15% that does happen in ways that surprise us with our ability to turn the situation around.

To achieve this competency, you don't need anything more complicated than a pen and paper or a hard-bound journal. I personally prefer a computer so that I can include photos, images, audio, and video clips to enhance my experience, both in the here and now and for future reference.

The sooner you record your status, the better. This will prevent you from forgetting exactly what happened.

Finally, to get the most out of journaling, it helps to have a plan around what you want to write about. To help you get started I suggest you complete the following assignment. This assignment will allow you to delve into journaling with a purpose that supports the remainder of this competency.

IDEAS FOR MASTERING THIS COMPETENCY

Figure 5: The Life Satisfaction Scale

Terrible 1 -- 2 -- 3 -- 4 -- 5 -- 6 -- 7 -- 8 -- 9 -- 10 Ideal

Where are you on the scale?
Why aren't you lower on the scale?
What will it take to get higher on the scale?

Knowing how you are doing throughout the day is the first step in the process of intentional change. It allows you to determine such things as whether or not you are making progress, what is working and what is not working, and to begin to see what is going on inside and outside yourself when you are OK and when you are not OK.

To begin this personal observation process 1) decide how you will record your status (e.g., journal, diary, notebook, computer); 2) check your status three times per day and record your answers to the three questions on the "Life Satisfaction Scale"; 3) every night before you go to sleep, write down three things that went well during the day and why; and 4) use the Hassle Tracker (Table 6) to identify what is upsetting you on a consistent basis. Perform each of these status checks for at least seven consecutive days.

Use this guide or your journal to begin documenting all the people places and things you encounter in your day-to-day life that **consistently** make you upset. In Column 2, write down thinks things you typically think, feel and do in response to those things that are upsetting to you. As you do this exercise try to identify what things consistently make you upset. Record the patterns you discover in your journal.

Table 6
The Hassle Tracker

Write down the people, places and things that cause you to be upset. Record approximately when these things happen (Day/Time).	Record what you were thinking, feeling and doing as a consequence of the upsetting things you list in Column 1.

My Plan for Mastering Competency 1
How will I keep track of how I am doing relative to what I am trying to change or improve?

Competency 2
Communicate Effectively

The ability to communicate effectively is a key component in psychological resilience and in the ability to live a rational, productive, happy life. With this in mind, the focus of this section is on interpersonal communication, which is an exchange of information between you and one or more people.

Effective interpersonal communication is required to successfully start and maintain relationships, ask for what you want, understand what others want, resolve differences, and solve problems. It is both an art and a science that depends on a skill set that includes both verbal and non-verbal messages (made up of words, phrases, stories, tones, facial expressions, gestures and body language), timing, attentive listening, the capacity to regulate emotion in yourself, and the ability to recognize and understand the verbal and nonverbal cues and emotions of the person you're communicating with.

By learning these skills you can learn to communicate in ways that are effective. By effective, I mean that the messages you send will be clearly understood and will help you to develop stronger relationships, reduce the likelihood of conflict, cause people to trust and like you more, and be persuasive—which means you will, in effect, get more of what you want out of life. Perhaps most importantly you will be able to better connect with your family, friends, coworkers, and casual acquaintances.

Specifically, the communication skills introduced and explained under this competency include how to prepare for, initiate, maintain, and end a conversation; ensure that your body language supports your verbal messages; listen attentively; regulate your emotions during a conversation; say hard thing things without causing hard feelings; and overcome objections or challenges, including pressure to do things that are not consistent with your personal values. I will also provide you with some important techniques that are helpful in becoming a great conversationalist.

Preparing to Communicate

If you were raised by parents who were good communicators and were around siblings who followed suit, it's likely that you naturally have good skills. If, on the other hand, your parents weren't so good at expressing themselves or, for some reason (you devoted an inordinate amount of time to video games) you did not communicate much or you were raised without exposure to siblings or had few friends, it's quite possible that you don't have great skills. The good news here is that you can develop skills in this area just like you can in any other endeavor. This requires preparation and practice. Put another way, if you want to be a good communicator you must learn to think and do the things good communicators think and do. My experience is that anyone who wants to do this can. In fact, many times individuals who have weaknesses in this area actually find, with the right training, that communication becomes their strong suit.

To prepare yourself to communicate effectively I suggest that you put together an interesting story about yourself, and a number of interesting facts that you can refer to as conversation starters or "filler." Your personal story should include things about you that are interesting. Ask someone you know and trust to help you with this. If you can't think of anything about you that is interesting then develop some hobbies or skills that make your story more interesting. Everyone is born without any experience—as a blank slate. Those who decide to develop their talents and do interesting things become interesting people. Those who choose not to do this are less interesting. Fortunately, it's never too late to reinvent yourself, start a hobby, or develop a new skill. My brother-in-law makes pies. The cooks in our family talk about how great Jim's pies are. Frankly, his first pie many years ago wasn't that good. The pies he makes now are delicious. I dabble in training and riding horses; I have ridden my bicycle several hundred miles; I was in Judo for many years; I have written some books; I have traveled around the world. None of this came naturally. Just as Jim decided to learn how to make pies, I learned how to ride a bike, ride horses, navigate my way around the world, etc. My wife Priscilla loves music and can talk to anyone about popular culture. Instead of making excuses here like, "Nothing about me is interesting," make your life interesting. If you are not willing to do this then make up some very good and very interesting excuses for not doing interesting things in your life. I have known individuals who have become somewhat interesting conversationalists based on of all the many ways they find to excuse themselves from self-improvement or change.

In addition to creating an interesting story about yourself, I suggest that you accumulate some "interesting" facts that you can use to enhance your verbal communication. I like to do this in "3s" because of a principle that I will explain laterwhen I discuss how to have a difficult conversation. For example, decide on and memorize what will become (because you will make it so) "your" three favorite quotes, current events, trivia, stories, songs, books, actors, historical events, places to visit, etc. I also think it's helpful to build a decent vocabulary. I have done this in the past by memorizing a new word each day and trying to use it in a conversation with at least one person.

Taken together, an interesting story about yourself and a number of facts that you have committed to memory will be very useful as you converse verbally. Frankly, very few people are not willing to listen to a good story, an interesting quote, or some popular trivia. If you have these things at the tip of your tongue, those you are communicating with may even think you are intelligent or witty or clever or downright cool.

Now that you are prepared and armed with some interesting information about yourself and the world around you—including some popular trivia—it's important to understand how to start, maintain, and end a conversation. Although it can seem like a giant chasm that must be crossed to go from being an ineffective communicator to becoming an effective communicator, once you have some idea about how to break the ice and keep things flowing, you will notice that your confidence will begin to soar. This is because of the principle that is stated in the ancient proverb that says, "If ye are prepared, ye shall not fear."

Starting a Conversation

For most of us, breaking the ice is the most difficult part in starting a conversation. However, after the ice is broken, everything else tends to come much easier.

Although I will provide you with some ideas here, if you use a common internet search engine like Google and type in the words "how to start a conversation," you will get about 425,000,000 results in 0.35 seconds (I just did it). In other words, this is a very popular topic and there are countless resources on how to do it. Another resource I just tried was toward.youtube.com. When I typed in "how to start a conversation," I got 759,000 hits. Again, because there is so much interest in this topic, you should be able to find useful resources. This should also tell you that there are many people who are struggling with communication and who are looking for help, so you should not feel alone in this challenge.

The "3s" of Conversation

When is the best time and what are the best ways to start a conversation? Frankly, there is no time like the present to start a conversation. This is because there really isn't a perfect time, and if you wait for a "perfect time," your opportunity may be lost. To avoid this, I suggest that you prepare to start a conversation by deciding on a number of different questions that you will use, depending on the circumstance, to break the ice and start communicating. Ideally, these questions should be about things you are familiar with or at least interested in. This is because it's easier to be present and to stay present when you are talking about something you know something about.

If you follow my recommendation to prepare by coming up with the "3s" I mentioned above, you could start conversations that relate to the material you have prepared. That way, you will have plenty of follow-up material when you start the conversation.

For example,
What is your favorite quote?
Who is your favorite actor?
What is your favorite movie?
What is the worst movie you have ever seen?
Who is your favorite band?
What is your favorite song?
Who is your favorite athlete?
What is your favorite athletic team? Or, do you follow any kind of sport?
What is your favorite sports car? What kind of car do you drive?
What is your favorite TV show or movie of all time?
What is your favorite book?
What is the last book you read? Do you recommend it?
What is your favorite Aesop's Fable?

Other questions that make great starters are as follows:
What do you think of the weather? What is your favorite season?
Do you have pets? Are you a cat person or a dog person?
Who is your favorite super hero?
If you had a super power, what would it be? Why that one?

How often do you exercise? What is your favorite type of exercise?

What do you think of abortion or euthanasia?

What do you think of religion or God?

What do you think of politics?

Do you play any sports?

How is your day?

Do you know what time it is?

What is your opinion about (choose something)?

What kind of cell phone do you have, and why did you choose that one?

Do you know any good places to eat?

Have you seen any good movies lately?

What do you think of school?

Where do you go to school?

What do you think of your teacher?

Do you have siblings?

Where are your ancestors from?

What does your name mean?

Do you speak more than one language?

Where were you born?

Where did you grow up?

What do you do on the weekends?

What is your favorite food, or drink, or meal of the day?

How are you with money?

What is the last thing you regret buying?

What is the last thing you returned to the store?

Are there any foods that you dislike or will not eat?

Are there any foods that you would like to try?

What is your favorite desert, or ice cream, or cake, or pie?

What is your favorite place to eat Mexican, or Italian, or Chinese, or fast food?

What did you have for breakfast, or lunch, or dinner?

What inspires you?

What do you wish you could do but don't believe you can?

If you saw something committing an illegal act like robbing a house or shoplifting, what would you do?

What would you do if you saw someone cheating on someone you know?

What do you want your life to stand for?

If you could fix one problem in the world, what would it be?

What would you do about this problem?

What are your most important values?

What are the main things that motivate you or bring you joy and satisfaction?

What are your two best moments you have experienced in the past ten years?

What three things would you do if you won a 200 million dollar lottery?

What are your greatest strengths/abilities/traits/things you do best?

What are at least two things I can start doing/do more often that use your strengths and bring you joy?

What are at least two things you can start thinking that will bring you greater happiness?

What are at least two things you'd like to stop doing or do as little as possible?

If a miracle occurred and your life was just like you wanted it to be, what would be different?

Have you ever had a "wake up call" you didn't answer?

What do you do to relax?

Who is your favorite person to be with?

Which historical figure would you like to meet?

If you were stranded on a deserted island and you could have only three things, what would they be?

Whom would you want to be stranded with?

Do you like video games? What are your favorite games? Why?

Do you believe in luck? Are you lucky?

Do you play board games? What is your favorite board game?

What is your favorite cause or charity? Do you donate time or money?

Have you ever been in a car wreck? Have you ever gotten a speeding or a parking ticket?

If you could live anywhere you wanted, where would it be?

Do you prefer to live in the city or the country?

What is the best thing that happened to you this year?

What is the worst thing that happened to you this year?

Do you shower? Do you sing in the shower? What is your favorite shampoo?

What would you do if you only had a week to live?

What is the first thing you do when you wake up in the morning?

What's the last thing you do every day before bed?

What is the craziest thing you have ever done?

What is your favorite thing to do on your birthday?

What is your favorite time of day?

What is your favorite day of the week?

What is your favorite holiday?

What is your favorite subject in school?

What's your favorite part of the school year?

Where do you see yourself ten years from now?

Obviously, there is an almost infinite number of questions that can kick off a conversation. As I suggested above, I recommend that you pick questions that relate to things you are interested in.

Another approach I have used that is easy to remember is to give someone a genuine compliment. For example, I might say, "Wow, those are cool jeans! Where did you get them?" or, "I really like your car. Is it fast? What kind of a sound system does it have? Where did you get it?"

Frankly, people like complements and love to talk about themselves, so anything you can compliment about a person or something they own or are involved with is a great icebreaker.

If someone is disrespectful when you ask a question, say something like, "Nice one," and then ask the person if he or she is OK. Or, you could ask something like, "What does that even mean?" These are ways of countering the apparent rejection while putting the pressure back on the person who was disrespectful in a respectful way that may actually start a conversation.

How To Keep a Conversation Going

There are many ways to keep a conversation going. In my opinion, the easiest approach to learn and apply is what I call the "WH-Question" approach. This approach involves remembering and applying any number of the questions: Who, What, When, Where, Why, How, and How often? These questions can be used at any point in a conversation to get things started or to keep things moving. For example, if you meet someone at a social event you can ask the questions: How is it going, or How are you? What are you up to? When did you get here? Where are you from? Why are you here? How did you get here? How often do you come to this place?

The best way to keep a conversation going with WH-questions is to listen carefully to the person you are conversing with and, at the right moment, latch onto any topic that he or she brings up in response to your icebreaker question. By latching on, I mean begin to apply the WH-questions to any topic that breaks the ice. Some examples of applying WH-Questions to some of the conversation starter questions I provided above are as follows:

What do you think of the weather?

- How are you with weather like this?
- What do you usually do on a day like this?
- Where are you from originally?
- What is the weather like where you are from?
- Why did you end up here?
- When did you get here?
- How did you get here: car, airplane, or bus?
- What is your favorite season?

Do you have any pets? Whether they have pets or not, you can ask the following WH questions.

- How are you with pets?
- What are your favorite pets?
- How many pets do you own (or have you owned)?
- What kind of pets do you own (or have you owned)?
- Where do you typically get your pets?

- Have you ever gotten pets from a shelter?

- What is your favorite pet story?

- What is your worst pet story?

Do you work out?

- How long have you been working out?

- What kind of workouts do you do?

- How long and how many days per week?

- Where do you like to work out?

- What is your overall workout goal?

- What is your favorite workout story?

- What is your worst workout experience?

- What kind of exercise training do you have?

Do you like sports?

- What is your favorite sport to play?

- Why do you like this sport? What do you like most about it?

- How did you learn this sport?

- Who is your hero in this sport?

- When did you start participating in this sport?

- How long have you participated?

- What is your best story/memory?

- What is your worst story/memory?

- What is your favorite sport to watch?

- Who is your favorite team?

- Why is this your favorite team?

Who is your favorite super hero?

- Why is this your favorite character?

- What do you like most about this character?

- What are your favorite super powers?

- If you had a super power, what would it be? Oh that's interesting, why that one?

- What super hero would you be if you got your wish?
- When did you first start getting into this character?
- How has this character influenced your life?
- If you could be in a relationship with a super hero, with whom would it be?

Are you following any current events?

- What about that event captured your interest?
- When did you become interesting?
- How has it impacted you?
- What should I know about it?
- Which current events are you most worried about?
- Which current events are you most excited about?

Are you a history buff?

- Which historical events do you find most interesting?
- If you could be anyone in history, who would you be? Why?
- What do you think are the most important events in history?
- If you had a time machine, would you go back in time?
- What place in time would you travel to? Why?

Are you interested in politics?

- What do you like and dislike about politics?
- Who is your favorite politician?
- Who was your favorite president?
- What impact has politics had on you and those you know?
- Which political party do you support?
- How do you support the party?
- What is it about this party that is so attractive to you?
- Why do many people have so much trouble discussing politics?

One of the easiest strategies is to have follow-up questions to your icebreaker—the conversation starters above. For example, if the person responds to a question or compliment about their car, follow up with some questions about where they got the car, why they selected the car over others, how much it cost, whether or not it's reliable, and so on. Similarly, if you ask what a person is most scared of, you can follow up with questions about ghosts, and graveyards, and horror movies, and so on. If you ask sensitive questions about something like politics, you can follow up with their party affiliation, what they think about war, gay marriage, abortion, etc.

Another tactic that I use once I get a conversation going is to focus on a topic the person I am talking to seems to be interested in. I do one of three things: ask a question about it, make a statement about it, and/or relate it to one of my own experiences. For example, if the person is interested in music I can ask a question like: Who is your favorite band? I can make a statement like "My favorite band is... Finally, I can relate it to one of my experiences about my favorite band like "I saw my favorite band in concert in Los Angeles." You can use this technique over and over again by simply tracking closely what the other person is saying, and then repeating the process of questioning, commenting, and relating back to your own experiences.

Another important thing to do when trying to keep a conversation going is to ask open-ended questions instead of questions that allow for yes or no answers. For example, asking open-ended questions like "What do you think of politics? or "What are your best memories? gives the person you are talking to a lot of latitude for responding and further discussions. If, however, you simply ask closed-ended questions like "Are you a Republican or Democrat? or "Do you have any good memories?" the answers will be very brief like "Republican" or "No," respectively.

Finally, perhaps my favorite "keeping it going" communication technique is often referred to as "Interesting, Tell Me More." This approach requires good listening skills that can be readily understood and applied using the following formulaic approach, which is often called "active listening" or "mirroring." I teach these techniques to couples when I start marriage counseling because without them, a session usually turns into a free for all. I am not sure of the origins of this technique, but the person who taught it to me was the author of the book "Getting the Love you Want," Harvel Hendrix. This approach involves three steps.

- Listen carefully to the person you are conversing with, and at appropriate points in the conversation, stop and paraphrase what the person is saying. This is an art and will take some practice, which will be well worth the effort given how powerful the technique is.

- After paraphrasing, check with the person you are talking with to determine whether your paraphrase is accurate by simply asking the question, "Is that right?" or "Am I getting it?"

- Once you check in and confirm that you understood what was being said—you are getting it—ask the question, "Is there more about that?" This question tells the person you are conversing with that you are interested in what is being said and you'd like to hear more."

This three-step approach can be supplemented by expressions like "that's cool," or "that makes sense," or "wow, are you serious," or "interesting, tell me more," and so on. These bits of conversation further solidify that you are listening, which, in most cases, will cause the person you are talking with to want to spend more time with you. After all, who doesn't want to hang out with someone who is genuinely interested in what they have to say. Frankly, it's very flattering to know that another person is really tracking on your ideas and wants to know more about a topic you are interested in.

I know this technique works because I do this in my clinics day after day while my clients tell me all kinds of interesting things about their lives. Sometimes they share things they have never told another person. At some point during my sessions, I ask my clients about how things are going and what about the process is helpful. More often than not they will say something like "it's just good to have someone who will listen without judging me." This nonjudgmental approach to listening can be used in almost any conversation, and the more you do it, the better you will get at keeping a conversation going.

Ending a Conversation

Ending a conversation seems like a no-brainer; you just stop talking or say goodbye and walk away, right? Although this is literally true, it's not very tactful or effective to end a conversation without some kind of transitional comment that is often preceded by a nonverbal cue. Furthermore, ending a conversation is an essential part of effective communication and is an essential ingredient in getting along with others.

One good way of ending a conversation is looking for a pause in the conversation and then inserting a transitional compliment like, "Wow, it's been good catching up with you, and it was great to hear that you are doing so well in school or at work." You can give a reason or an excuse like, "Darn, I need to go to another meeting," or "I need to finish some chores," or "I've gotta go finish my homework," or "I need to get back to the office as I am working on a deadline," or "I hate to say goodbye, but I need to finish this project," or "I have to give someone a call," or "I need to call to make an appointment." You can summarize what is being said and then, at the end of the summary, say, "I really enjoyed catching up." Finally, you can give nonverbal cues with your body language, such as standing up if you are sitting down, shaking hands, or opening a door, or looking at your watch and so on.

IDEAS FOR MASTERING THIS COMPETENCY

The "Conversational Communication Planner" outlined here is designed to help you improve your conversational skills and overcome anxiety associated with communicating with other individuals or groups. Please complete each section of the planner as instructed.

1. **Prepare to be an effective conversationalist and/or presenter. Do this by 1) writing an interesting story about yourself and 2) identifying a number of facts that you can use as a part of your conversations and presentations.**

    *   The points you should include in your story can include anything that others may be interesting. If you can't think of anything that you have done that is interesting, start engaging in activities and hobbies that others will find interesting. You can find ideas by using a search engine like Google.

- The "interesting facts" that you identify should include things in "3s," like three favorite bands, songs, authors, movies, places you want to visit, quotes, historical figures, animals, etc.

2. **Develop an extensive list of things you can say to "start" a conversation or presentation. You can find this information online using Google and/or YouTube.**

   - Watch at least two videos per day on YouTube that pertain to this topic. Either download or make an electronic file that includes copies of the URLs to your favorite videos.

   - Carry several of these starters with you at all times.

   - Practice them several times per day for the first seven days (practice in front of the mirror at least twice per day).

   - If you want to have some fun and increase your confidence further, you can practice in front of someone who is making fun of you and laughing at you. This can help desensitize you to distractions that may throw off you concentration when you are trying to communicate effectively.

3. **Develop a list of things you can say to keep a conversation going. You can find this information online using Google and/or YouTube.**

   - Watch at least two videos per day on YouTube that pertain to this topic. Either download or make an electronic file that includes copies of the URLs to your favorite videos.

   - Carry several of these follow-up ideas with you at all times.

   - Practice them several times per day for the first seven days (practice in front of the mirror at least twice per day).

   - Once again, if you want to liven this up a bit you can practice in front of someone who is making fun of you and laughing at you.

4. **Develop a list of things you can say to tactfully end a conversation. You can find this information online using Google and/or YouTube.**

   - Watch at least two videos per day on YouTube that pertain to this topic. Either download or make an electronic file that includes copies of the URLs to your favorite videos.

   - Carry several of these wrap-up ideas with you at all times.

   - Practice them several times per day for the first seven days (practice in front of the mirror at least twice per day).

   - Practice them in front of someone who is making fun of you and laughing at you.

5. **Develop rational thoughts and tell yourself stories that help you feel calm before, during, and after you talk to individuals or groups. You will do this**

by 1) identifying thoughts and stories that upset you before, during, and after speaking to individuals or groups (Column 1) and 2) formulating new thoughts and stories you will tell yourself, INSTEAD OF those things you think that make you feel nervous when you speak (Column 2). You will tell yourself these new stories to feel calm before, during, and after you speak.

Thoughts and Stories that Make Me Anxious Before, During, and After Speaking	Thoughts and Stories I Will Tell Myself that Will Make Me Confident and Calm Before, During, and After Speaking

6. **When you are in a conversation with another person, Practice Active Listening by applying the following four-step process:** 1) listen carefully to what is being said, 2) paraphrase back to the person you are listening to what you hear him or her say, 3) ask if what you heard (based on what you said in the paraphrase) was correct, and 4) ask if there is anything else he or she wants to share on the topic you are discussing.

Making this listening process a habit will make you a very popular, very effective communicator. This is because people love to be listened to and validated. When you accurately track on what people are saying as evidenced by the accuracy of what you paraphrase back to them, they "feel" that you are listening and are interested.

NOTE: Make a list of things you should remember when talking and listening to other individuals or groups. This list will serve as a ready reference of useful information that you can refer to before you engage in a conversation or give a presentation.

My Plan for Mastering Competency 2

How will I improve my interpersonal communication knowledge and skills?

Competency 3
Rationally Define and Solve Problems

Life is difficult! After four decades of marriage and raising children, I understand this first hand. Life is also difficult in the workplace. Having worked as a clinician and at the highest levels of local and national organizations, I've encountered problems that I never imagined when I received my doctorate degree and entered the workforce in 1982. Frankly, I've "been there and done that" when it comes to solving many difficult individual and interpersonal problems. Through all of this and more, I have evolved from someone who once avoided problems to a person who sees problems as ripe opportunities for personal and interpersonal growth and development. In fact, as a psychotherapist and public health professional, I make my living solving problems.

This is not to say I enjoy problems. It is, however, to say that learning to rationally conceptualize and solve problems can bring about a great deal of personal satisfaction.

Through all my personal and professional experience I have learned some important lessons and principles about Competency 3. Perhaps the most important lesson I have learned is that those individuals who become good at solving problems are highly valued by society, and they experience a greater sense of well-being. This is because they understand some universal truths about the nature of problems, including that facts that 1) all people have problems; 2) life is not fair in that many problems we experience are caused by circumstances outside our control; 3) problems present opportunities for learning and development; 4) complaining or getting angry is not an effective way of solving problems; 5) being patient, rational, and innovative helps when problems are not readily resolved; and 6) learning to effectively solve problems reduces the stress that accompany them.

I once heard a story that has helped me remain patient when dealing with difficult problems. And, given the nature of the work I do, it's not unusual to be challenged on a rather frequent basis with difficult problems that can, at first, seem overwhelming.

After working on a project in China for a period of time, I decided to hire a driver to take me to visit the Great Wall. On the way to the Wall my driver suggested I stop in a small village and witness the making of different types of pottery. While looking over the pottery, I remarked that I loved one of the vases that had the images of running horses painted on the outside. When the person who was showing me the piece learned that I was born in the "Year of the Horse," he told me a story that convinced me that I should purchase the vase as a reminder of the principle taught in the story.

Although the story may not be true, my guide told it as if it was, so I am including it here because it illustrates my point. She said that in her village there lived a Zen master who loved horses. One day as he was meditating in the woods near the village, he saw a horse grazing nearby. The master, knowing something about horses, was able to catch the animal and bring it back to the village. When he arrived at the village and corralled the horse, many villagers stopped by the master's house and remarked, "Master, you are very lucky, you captured a horse." In response the master said, "I will wait and see."

The next day the master's newly captured horse broke free and was lost again in the woods. When the villagers found out, they stopped by the master's house and said, "Master, you are very unlucky, your horse has escaped." Again, the master said, "I will wait and see." The next day the master's son went out into the woods in search of the lost horse. After searching for a while he found the horse grazing in a meadow. The master's son was able to catch the horse and return it to his father, who then put the horse in a more secure corral. When the villagers heard the news they gathered at the master's home and said, "You are very lucky that your son was able to recapture the horse." As usual, the Zen master said, "I will wait and see."

The next day, the master's son was bucked off the horse when he tried to ride it. When he hit the ground, he broke his leg. When the villagers heard what happened, many visited the master's home and said he was unlucky because his son's leg was now broken. As always, the wise Zen master said, "I will wait and see."

The next day, a group of Chinese soldiers came to the village recruiting young men the age of the master's son to go to a serious battle across the Great Wall against the Mongolian army. That evening, after the dust settled, some villagers stopped by the master's house and said, "You are very lucky because your son broke his leg and did not have to go fight in the terrible battle." And as always, the master responded, "I will wait and see."

I have heard similar stories in many different countries. It is the story of "letting go" or embracing instead of fighting against the things that happen to us as a part of living. The Zen master understood this concept very well. He knew that declaring a problem as lucky or unlucky was unwise because he also understood that we, as humans, do not have control over what happens in our day-to-day lives. Instead of fighting the realities of life, the master simply accepted the events of each day.

This is all to say that, in spite of your best efforts, you will have problems. And fighting against, instead of learning to be patient and adapt to, these realities only brings us frustration. Embracing them, even when the events are very painful, allows us to feel peace in the midst of our sometimes chaotic lives. This is especially relevant when trying to understand and solve difficult problems.

Another important truth about problems is reflected in a quote by Henry David Thoreau: "There are a thousand hacking at the branches of evil to one who is striking at the root." This quote reminds me that before I can solve a problem, I must understand the nature of the problem and what's causing it, i.e., the root cause. Without an understanding of what the problem is and what's causing it, efforts to resolve the issue are oftentimes misguided and ineffective.

There are many good approaches to problem solving. The approach I recommend is called the "Problem Solving Planner" or the PSP.

IDEAS FOR MASTERING THIS COMPETENCY

Below are two different approaches to problems solving. The first approach requires that you make a list of the problems you are currently struggling with and then ask yourself a number questions that are designed to help you think strategically about the problem, its causes, and what you need to think and do differently to address the root causes and overcome the problem.

The second approach uses what is called the "Problem Solving Planner" or PSP. This tool will guide you through a step-by-step process that helps you understand the nature and determinants of the problem before you develop a plan to address it.

List the most difficult problems you are currently struggling with. Problems are discrepancies between the way things are in your life and the way you want them to be.

> Problem A:
>
> Problem B:
>
> Problem C:

How do you feel when you experience this problem: embarrassed, guilty, angry, sad, incompetent, afraid, anxious, hopeless, unhappy, disappointed, pessimistic, frustrated, regretful, lonely, inferior, panicky, worthless?

> Problem A:
>
> Problem B:
>
> Problem C:

What do you think or do that contributes to each problem and the negative feelings? This will help you isolate those things you have control over.

> Problem A:
>
> Problem B:
>
> Problem C:

What can you think or do differently that will help you solve the problem and eliminate the negative emotions? That is, to 1) help you achieve your goals and 2) feel the way you want to feel? These thoughts and actions should fit the valid thought system in Tables 7a and 7b.

> Problem A:
>
> Problem B:
>
> Problem C:

What will you do, how often, for how long, and what support/resources will you need?

> Problem A:
>
> Problem B:
>
> Problem C:

Document what you did and did not do, and how you feel as a consequence.

> Problem A:
>
> Problem B:

Problem C:

*Assess the rationality of your thinking by asking yourself whether the above thoughts and actions have been demonstrated as effective in helping others solve the kinds of problems you are trying to overcome.

As was mentioned above, the second approach you can use to develop this competency is a problem-solving tool called the PSP. This tool has two phases.

Phase I the PSP (Table 7a) directs you to 1) identify the problem, 2) define the problem, 3) investigate to determine the causes and possible solutions, 4) decide which causes you will address and which action steps you will take to alleviate these causes, and 5) establish a schedule for monitoring progress and getting feedback that can be used to improve the strategy. In Phase II (Table 7b), you put the information together to make up your intervention strategy.

Table 7a
Phase I — The Problem Solving Planner

Understanding the Problem

Step 1: Identify the Problem

A problem is a "gap" between what should be happening and what is actually happening in your life. For example, if you want to earn a raise but you are getting passed over, you have a problem.

Step 2: Define the Problem

Clearly stating the problem you plan to work on is essential to focus on what it is that you plan to change.

Step 3: Investigate to Determine the Causes and Possible Solutions

If you can determine what is causing the problem, then you will be able to focus your attention on the causes rather than the symptoms.

Step 4: Decide Which Causes to Address and Which Steps to Take to

Alleviate Them

Once you know what the problem is, and what is causing it, you will be able to select the appropriate action steps to address each cause.

Step 5: Establish a Schedule for Monitoring Progress and Getting

Feedback

You must follow up to ensure that each action step is executed.

As indicated above, in Phase II of the PSP you put your strategy together. The matrix that follows will help you do this in a systematic way. In Column 1, you list what you perceive to be the causes of the problem. In Column 2, you describe the action steps you will take in connection with each cause. Finally, in Column 3 you record information about when the action steps will be completed.

Table 7b
Phase II — The Problem Solving Planner

Problem Resolution Plan		
Causes to Be Addressed	Action Steps	When Actions Are Completed

My Plan for Mastering Competency 3
How will I rationally solve the problems I encounter on a daily basis?

Competency 4
Develop and Implement a Personal Improvement Plan

A wise person once said, "By small and simple things, great things (for good or bad) come to pass." For example, to improve my vocabulary I once decided to learn every day for a year a new word and how to use it. This allowed me to learn and apply 365 new words. Another good example is when one of my patients was bemoaning the fact that, after 22 years of marriage, he was 45 pounds overweight. If you think about this, this individual only put on two pounds the first year, and four pounds by the end of his second year of marriage. I am sure he and his wife, who was now concerned about his weight, barely noticed the four pounds. However, because he continued at a two-pound average increase of weight of two pounds per year, he was now sitting in my office 45 pounds over weight. Obviously, had he come to me at the end of the first year, getting back down to weight would have been a reasonably simple task—at least much easier than losing the 45 pounds which, by the way, he did accomplish using this system described here.

My clinical work has demonstrated that those who consistently engage in self-improvement activities that are designed to bring balance to their lives like exercise, eating right, meditation, and healthy socializing tend to have a greater capacity to overcome life challenges, including such things as the death of a loved one, divorce, financial setbacks, injury or illness, getting laid off at work, etc. Conversely, those who don't put in the time to balance their lives tend to be more reactionary and less likely to respond rationally in the face of life's inevitable challenges. With this in mind, I encourage my clients who are feeling out of control to develop a plan to bring some balance back into their lives. That is, I encourage them to become proactive instead of reactive. To make my point I often tell them a story about a TV ad that I saw many years ago. The ad, which was designed to sell oil filters, featured a mechanic who made the point that it's better to change your oil and use a good filter than experience major engine problems. This was illustrated by the mechanic when he held up the oil filter and said "pay me now" (for the filter) or "pay me later" (for major engine repair), at which time he pointed to a car on a lift in his garage.

I believe the same principle applies to people. That is, if we don't practice prevention, we will pay a bigger price down the road. Further, because we are multi-dimensional, I believe it's important that we pay attention to all dimensions of ourselves to ensure good health and well-being.

As much as anything, this idea has to do with living a balanced life. By practicing prevention across the different dimensions of your being, including your physical, emotional, intellectual (mental), social, and spiritual dimensions, you will attain balance which will, in turn, reduce major problems down the road. A brief description of each dimension, along with some specific examples of why it's important to proactively build and maintain balance across each dimension of resilience, is provided below.

Physical Dimension: The effects of not consistently paying attention to this dimension are oftentimes more obvious than the other dimensions. For example, if a young adult who is at an ideal weight at age 20 puts on two pounds per year for 40 years, they will be 80 pounds overweight by the time they reach 60. Although the first year the two additional pounds don't seem like much at all, the consistent increase amounts to a lot. Along the same lines, if we don't apply self-restraint on a regular basis in terms of how much we eat, we can put on excess pounds; and most adults know, by sad experience, the heavy price they must pay to overcome unwanted body weight.

As I mentioned earlier, it is important to our physical dimension that we exercise on a regular basis. For instance, exercise physiologists have determined that if we exercise aerobically (walk, jog, skate, bike, etc.) most days each week, for at least twenty minutes per session, we will experience a positive "training effect" on our heart, lungs, and blood vessels. The subsequent benefit of such a training effect can also serve to illustrate the interrelationship between the dimensions of our well-being spoken of earlier. That is, in addition to receiving physical benefits such as reduced heart disease, lower percent body fat, lower blood pressure, lower blood cholesterol, and so on, those who engage in aerobic exercise on a regular basis also receive mental health benefits such as improved self-esteem, enhanced perception of body image, decreased depression and anxiety, as well as social benefits such as a fuller social life because of an enhanced appearance and an improved attitude and zest for living.

In fact, researchers in California (Belloc and Breslow) who studied the lives of 7,000 men and women found a relationship between physical well-being and years of life lived to adherence to seven basic practices: (a) sleeping seven to eight hours each night, (b) eating three meals a day at regular times with little snacking, (c) eating breakfast every day, (d) maintaining desirable body weight, (e) avoiding excessive alcohol consumption, (f) getting regular exercise, and (g) not smoking. This report also indicated that men at age 45 who follow three or fewer of these practices, can expect to live to 67; however, men in the same age group who follow six to seven of these practices could expect to live to 78. Similarly, women age 45, who follow three or fewer of these practices, can expect to live to age 74, while women who abide six or seven of these practices can expect to live to 81.

A more recent example of how being proactive about our health can produce benefits is born out in a study released by a Scientific Committee in the United States in 2012. This committee reported that up to 50% of cancer in men and women could be prevented by taking a number of proactive steps, including: (a) reducing tobacco consumption, (b) increasing physical activity, (c) improving nutrition habits, (d) increasing evidence-based screening and early detection, (e) increasing proven cancer-preventive vaccinations, and (f) increasing protection against excessive UV light exposure of tobacco.

Emotional Dimension: The "pay me now or pay me later" concept can also be applied to mental health. Given that how you see yourself (self-esteem or self-image) is one of the best indicators of mental health, any threat to your perceived self-image is a threat to your emotional well-being and happiness. Furthermore, given that self-image is essentially the outcome of a succession of failures and successes in thinking rationally, each time we choose to think rationally about ourselves, our image of self improves. This means if you are suffering from negative self-image, you can take proactive steps—by thinking and doing rational things—to improve your self-image.

Another threat to a rational image that illustrates how the "pay me now or later" construct applies to the emotional dimension of our resilience has to do with the interrelationship between our values and our personal behavior. For example, it has been demonstrated that individuals who consistently behave in a manner that deviates from their core values experience a more negative perception of themselves—a less rational self-image. With this in mind, I encourage my clients to clarify their personal values and take steps to ensure that their thoughts and behaviors are consistent with their core beliefs and values.

Intellectual Dimension: Development or lack of development of your intellect also plays a role in happiness and well-being. If you don't "pay now" by consistently studying and assimilating new and diverse information—particularly in our highly specialized and technological society—you will likely pay the price later, manifested by under- or unemployment or the need for major retraining (the overhaul). Because we live in an information age where the proliferation of information is occurring at an unprecedented rate, one of the most important personal resiliency activities you can engage in on a regular basis is self-directed learning.

Social Dimension: Without a doubt, our social development or adeptness is key to health and well-being. If you don't "pay the price" to learn and practice good social skills, you may struggle in your relationships with family members, peers, and employers. The costs associated with not acquiring these skills can include poor relationships, the inability to make and keep friends, marital problems, and being passed over for desirable jobs or promotions, to mention a few. This dimension is of particular concern in modern society where effective face-to-face communication is rapidly being replaced by social technologies, and where the virtual worlds of video gaming are being substituted for "real world" activities required to develop the social competence required to function effectively in one's personal and work life.

Spiritual Dimension: Considerable research in recent years has documented what the prophets and wise-men have passed down through the ages, which is, attention or lack of attention to our spiritual and character development dimension can and does have a measurable impact on health and happiness. If you don't meet your needs in this area through such things as serving others, meditation and prayer, reading inspirational literature, learning the difference between good and bad/right and wrong, and other things that have been documented to improve spiritual health and character development, you can become seriously spiritually malnourished and be unprepared when confronted with the life crises that we all encounter.

Multi-Dimensional Considerations: Taken together, the dimensions I have just described, if addressed appropriately on a consistent basis, can increase your personal resilience and, in turn, increase the likelihood that you will be happy, healthy, and effective in all that you do. It should be noted, however, that to attain and maintain balance, the pursuit of meeting these needs should always be looked at as a means to an end rather than an end in itself. Many people, who get stuck on being popular or attaining big muscles or earning a lot of money at the expense of developing all areas, lose perspective and become imbalanced in their approach to living. Although it is not a bad thing to focus attention on one area or another, balance across all of these dimensions should be considered the ideal means toward the end of becoming a healthy, happy individual, who has the drive and resiliency necessary to realize a vision of your highest and best self-image.

IDEAS FOR MASTERING THIS COMPETENCY

A simple way to incorporate resiliency into your daily life is illustrated in the Table 8, the "Daily Resiliency Routine Guide." Because small and simple steps over time can lead to great accomplishments, using this guide to set in place activities that you will do on a regularly scheduled basis to improve your resilience will, in turn, ensure that you are getting stronger and not weaker in each of the dimensions described above.

Table 8
Daily Resiliency Routine Guide

My Daily Resiliency Routine		Mon	Tue	Wed	Thr	Fri	Sat	Sun
Specifically, what will I do on a daily basis to strengthen myself, when will I do it, where will I do it, and for how long will I do it?	Physical							
	Emotional							
	Intellectual (Mental)							
	Social							
	Spiritual							

Complete and begin implementing the "Personal Improvement Planning Matrix" in Table 9. This will help you clarify your personal goals, anticipate your problems, prepare to cope in rational ways, and increase your stress tolerance.

Table 9
Personal Improvement Planning Matrix

Use this guide to develop a plan for self-improvement. Review the plan every morning before you start your day and, every night before bed. This will help you in your efforts to consistently implement the plan!

These are my most important short and long-term goals. (I will review these daily.)	

Throughout the day, I will ask the following questions to determine whether or not my thoughts and actions are rational. Answering no to any of these questions indicates I am thinking or behaving irrationally.

Does the thought or action motivate me?

Does the thought or action encourage personal growth, emotional maturity, independence of thinking and action, and mental stability?

Does the thought or action help me feel good?

Does the thought or action help me achieve my goals?

Is the thought based on fact?

Has the thought or action been proven to help me achieve success?

My Daily Resiliency Routine		Mon	Tue	Wed	Thr	Fri	Sat	Sun
Specifically, what will I do on a daily basis to strengthen myself, when will I do it, where will I do it, and for how long will I do it?	Physical							
	Emotional							
	Intellectual (Mental)							
	Social							
	Spiritual							

Table 9
Personal Improvement Planning Matrix

These are the problems (or triggers) that typically cause difficulty or that I anticipate will cause the most stress during my day/week/month.	
Specifically, what will I think today that will help me overcome the items I listed in row 4?	
Specifically, what will I do today that will help me overcome the items I listed in row 4?	
Where can I spend time today and/or with whom can I spend time that will help me avoid temptation and achieve my goals?	

Obviously, you can use any number of formats for laying out a daily resiliency or "daily good habit" plan. There are also many tools, including Smartphone Apps, that can help you remember your plan and document your progress. One example of a simple, yet powerful plan is provided below in Table 10, "Daily Habits for Success and Increased Happiness."

Table 10
Daily Habits for Success and Increased Happiness

Remember to **DO** the things I have listed on my resilience plan (this assumes I have a resiliency plan).

Set and achieve at least one new small, measurable goal each day.

At the end of the day, ask myself, "What went well, and what went poorly today?" For each thing that did not go well, decide what I can think and do differently to increase the likelihood that this will not happen again. If I have no control over the situation, decide what I can think that will help me feel better about it.

Practice being grateful for my problems. When I experience a problem think to myself, "I am grateful for the problems I experienced today because, even though they are difficult and painful, each one of them presents an opportunity for personal growth and development." After all, this statement is true. When we experience and rationally cope with problems, we become stronger. A good example of this is weight lifting. When I lift weights, the muscles being taxed send a message to the brain that causes the flexed muscles to overcompensate and grow.

Each time I experience a problem or difficult life event I will think or do the following things, INSTEAD OF thinking or doing things that have upset me in the past:

_____

_____

Before going to bed, I will think of three things I can be grateful for and why.

My Plan for Mastering Competency 4

What will I do to build and maintain my resilience?

Competency 5
Create a Rational Personal Vision Statement

The quote I referenced in the introduction by Patrick Rothfuss has direct application to this competency. He said, "It's like everyone tells a story about themselves inside their own head. Always. All the time. That story makes you what you are. We build ourselves out of that story."

This quote reminds me that what we believe and think about ourselves and our future matters. It's so important to realize that no matter how hard we try to change, we cannot make significant progress until we begin to see ourselves in ways that are congruent with what we are trying to accomplish. Because of this, before you start changing you must make adjustments to the way you see yourself. If you don't, your subconscious will work against (resist) any goals that are not congruent with your self-perception.

This step will help you create a Rational Personal Vision Statement or RPVS. When completed, your RPVS will represent a rational (based on objective truth), optimistic, broad-based, mental model of your highest and best self with a bright and promising future.

As you will notice, as I explain the purpose and actions required to master Competency, 5, I will consistently use words like "see" and "visualize." This is because this competency and the competencies that follow include a number of activities that tap in to the right side of your brain—the hemisphere of your brain attributed to creativity. Ultimately, as you will begin to understand more fully when I introduce Competency 10, these right brain activities make your adoption of each competency more efficient and effective.

There are many benefits to developing a RPVS. For example, because your RPVS will articulate what your "ideal" self and life will look like, it will be easier to develop the goals, milestones, and strategies that will help you to realize your vision. A RPVS can also serve as a yardstick against which you can measure your current situation and your progress. Moreover, having a clear RPVS allows you to evaluate your values. If, for example, one of your values is integrity, you will know when you are compromising the fulfillment of your vision if you are acting without integrity. In other words, your RPVS will help guide the decisions you make and the directions you take.

Unlike a goal, once you have created it, your RPVS will rarely change. This is because it represents the very essence of who you are, who you want to become, and your reasons (your "WHYs") for the way you want to experience life and see yourself and your future. In short, you are manufacturing a new perspective. When you adopt this new perspective, you will start to notice that your thoughts and behaviors will begin to align with this new outlook which, in turn, will help you begin to leave behind your old, irrational ways of thinking and acting.

For obvious and rational reasons, your RPVS should have a positive tone. This is because the way you see yourself and your future impacts everything you think and do. Above all, it impacts your level of happiness and sense of serenity.

If your vision of self and your future is depicted in negative ways, your thoughts, behaviors, and state of happiness will be impacted negatively. Conversely, if you choose to think or do things that cause you to see yourself and your future in more positive ways (e.g., rationally viewing your future as promising and yourself as someone who has potential), your state of happiness and serenity will be influenced in a positive direction.

This is the basis for labeling a negative vision of yourself or your future as irrational. It's also why I can say that any effort you put into seeing yourself and your potential in a more positive light is a rational decision that will lead to increased happiness and success. This means that enduring happiness only comes to those who think and do what it takes to attain an image of themselves and their future that is rational, in that it increases rather than diminishes their sense of happiness, serenity, and overall success in life.

In addition to struggling with unhappiness, individuals who have an irrational view of themselves and their future have trouble achieving their goals because they are held back by their thinking, their perceived abilities, and their overall potential. According to self-image psychology, this means to do certain things you must see yourself as someone who can do those types of things. And, to see yourself doing certain things you must become the kind of person who does those things. With this in mind, the goal of Competency 5 is to help you overcome and change limiting beliefs about yourself, your abilities, and your future potential by creating an RPVS that will enable you to become the kind of person who does the kinds of things you want to do in life.

> *We become what we want to be by consistently being what we want to become. Character is a manifestation of what you are becoming.* Richard G Scott

I have successfully used the techniques described in this competency to help my clients 1) identify irrational beliefs about themselves and their future that limit their potential, and 2) replace these irrational beliefs with a Rational Personal Vision Statement that gives them a sense of hope and promise regarding their themselves and their potential. What is included here will help you begin manufacturing and testing your RPVS as a means of deciding how you want and need to see yourself to achieve your full potential.

As you begin this process it's useful to remember that there are two fundamental, but interrelated, aspects to a RPVS. They include designing a prototype RPVS that represents the best possible person you can become (given the real instead of the perceived limits on your potential) while living the best possible life you can live. More specifically, the RPVS you develop and evaluate should represent what you want to become, do, feel, think, own, associate with, and impact by some date in the future.

When you reflect on the final version of your RPVS, it should remind you that this final "highest and best" version of yourself and your future must be rational in that it helps you achieve your goals, feel the way you want to feel, solve your problems, and, above all, increase your state of happiness and sense of well-being. With this in mind, I have defined a RPVS as a conscious recognition and appraisal of your self and your future, grounded in the facts of reality, required to think and act in rational ways that promote personal and interpersonal growth and development, happiness, and serenity.

After using the techniques here to design and test and enhance the various elements that make up your RPVS, you will eventually decide on a final version that you will, in turn, work to mentally assimilate using the techniques described under Competency 10.

IDEAS FOR MASTERING THIS COMPETENCY

This assignment will guide you through a process of designing and testing a Rational Personal Vision Statement using the "Rational Personal Vision Statement Guide" and then, help you evaluate and refine your RPVS until you have decided on a final version. Once you have finalized your RPVS and identified what to add and what to take away from it, you can begin to choose to think and act in ways that will cause to realize everything you have outlined in your final RPVS.

Over time, as you decide to make additional changes, you will most likely need to revisit this statement. This is due to the fact that a necessary first step in true change requires making sure that you vision of self, or you self-image, is aligned with the things that you want to change about yourself. Once again, this is because you can't do certain things unless you become the kind of person who does those kinds of things.

The steps in this process are:

1. Review the following "Visioning Questions" to help you begin thinking about what you want to put in to your RPVS:

   - What inspires me? What do I want my life to stand for?

   - If I could fix one problem in the world what would it be? What would I do about this problem?

   - What are my most important values?

   - What are the main things that motivate me/bring me joy and satisfaction?

   - What are my two best moments I have experienced in the past ten years?

   - What three things would I do if I won a 200 million dollar lottery?

   - What are my greatest strengths/abilities/traits/things I do best?

   - What are at least two things I can start doing/do more often that use my strengths and bring me joy?

   - What are at least two things I can start thinking that will bring me greater happiness?

- What are at least two things I would like to stop doing or do as little as possible?

- If a miracle occurred and my life was just like I wanted it to be, what would be different?

Figure 6: Rational Personal Vision Statement Guide

Identify 10 pictures or images that represent what you want to BE, DO, GET. After you have finished this step, these images will represent your Rational Personal Vision Statement. Briefly 1) explain how each image represents something you want to BE (calm, successful, thin, on time, confident, faithful, disciplined, fun, trustworthy, etc.), DO (graduate from college, get married, travel around the world, write a book, etc.) and GET (a new car or home, great job, a boat, etc.). Then describe the reason WHY you want the things represented by each picture. After you have described how you want to see yourself and your future, and WHY, decide on 1 "Cue Word" that repre-

IMAGE 1	I want to...	The reasons WHY are...	Cue Word 1
IMAGE 2	I want to...	The reasons WHY are...	Cue Word 2
IMAGE 3	I want to...	The reasons WHY are...	Cue Word 3
IMAGE 4	I want to...	The reasons WHY are...	Cue Word 4
IMAGE 5	I want to...	The reasons WHY are...	Cue Word 5
IMAGE 6	I want to...	The reasons WHY are...	Cue Word 6
IMAGE 7	I want to...	The reasons WHY are...	Cue Word 7
IMAGE 8	I want to...	The reasons WHY are...	Cue Word 8
IMAGE 9	I want to...	The reasons WHY are...	Cue Word 9
IMAGE 10	I want to...	The reasons WHY are...	Cue Word 10

Use Figure 6, the "Rational Personal Vision Statement Guide" to a) identify pictures or images that represent the things you want to BEcome, Do or Get—taken together, these images will represent your ideal RPVS; b) briefly explain how each image represents something you want; c) describe the reason "WHY" you want these things; and d) after you have described what you want and WHY, decide on one "Cue Word" that represents each of the images making up your RPVS.

Use Figure 7, the "RPVS Rationality Guide" to evaluate and identify elements in your RPVS that are irrational.

Revise the irrational elements in your RPVS.

Repeat steps 2 and 3 until all elements in your RPVS are rational.

After completing this assignment move on to Competency 6. The following competencies will build on what you have done here by helping you refine, operationalize, and mentally assimilate your RPVS.

Figure 7: RPVS Rationality Guide

Ask each element (represented by an image and cue word) in your initial Rational Personal Vision Statement (RPVS) the following questions. If you answer no to any of these questions it's likely that the element you are considering is irrational. Revise the irrational elements until you can answer yes to every question. Feel free to add to or take away from the questions provided here.

If I fully adopt this element in my Rational Personal Vision Statement, will I:

- reach my full potential?

- become the kind of person I want to be?

- achieve my short- and long-term goals?

- learn from my past, prepare for my future, and live in the present?

- have the ability to think and act in terms of principles and not emotions?

- perceive myself as someone who is in control of my destiny?

- be able to solve my problems and ask others for help when I need it?

- feel secure about who I am, and not feel insecure when others question how I see myself and live my life?

- be able to evaluate what others think and feel against my own standards, and have the courage to act according to my own convictions, regardless of what others do or say?

- feel secure enough about my beliefs that I can change them in the face of new facts?

- be able to exercise self-control by stoping, thinking, and making rational decisions?

- look beyond the surface, find real meaning, and weigh the pros and cons of an event or issue?

- wait for things that I want even when this requires patience and delaying immediate gratification?

- keep trying, even when things don't go the way I would like them to?see myself as someone who is equal in value to others, rather than inferior or superior, while accepting differences in my abilities, socio-economic standing, and personal potential?

- respect and obey the laws that are rational in that they are fair and just?

- respect the dignity of all men and women, without respect to religion, race, or gender?

My Plan for Mastering Competency 5

How will I need to see myself to change or become the person I have created (through the elements of my RPVS)?

Competency 6
Set and Achieve Rational Goals

Competency 6 will guide you in setting and evaluating goals that are directly relevant to your RPVS. Specifically, the purposes of this competency are to help you 1) begin to operationalize (or implement) your RPVS by guiding you through the process of setting a single goal for each RPVS element, 2) evaluate the rationality of your goals, and 3) determine whether or not you are ready to achieve the goals you plan to set.

In short, goals are written statements that explain what you want to obtain or accomplish within a certain period of time. Good goals are specific, measurable, realistic, and stated in terms of a specific time period.

1) When I set goals I ask myself a set of questions, which I will refer to as the "Six Questions for Writing Goals." These questions help me operationalize what I plan to accomplish and by when.

2) Am I committed to this goal? If I am not committed to achieving the goal, it goes in the trash. If I am, the likelihood that I will achieve it is in the high 90% range. The point is, why set a goal if you are not committed to doing what it takes to achieve it?

3) What do I plan to accomplish? If I have a clear idea about what I am trying to accomplish, I will have a much better idea as to whether or not I can do what it takes to achieve the goal. If I do not have a precise understanding of where I am going and what I am going to do, I probably won't get there.

4) What will I need to do to prepare to achieve this goal? Getting prepared before I launch into a goal achieving mode is crucial. I typically spend at least ten days getting ready. This involves making a plan of action and visualizing how I will succeed before I begin the hard work of succeeding.

5) When will I start and finish? Setting a start and finish date is exciting for me. For example, if I plan to write a book, I spend several days deciding on what it will take to write the book and how long. In the case of the first version of this book, I gave myself from September 18, 2012, to January 2, 2013. Although it was a very ambitious schedule, it was realistic because I had already put together most of the material I wanted to write about.

6) What barriers may I encounter when trying to achieve this goal? Answering this question helps me anticipate the people, places, or things that may prevent me from achieving my goal. This information helps me plan what I will need to think and/or do differently to overcome barriers to successfully achieving my objective (Contingency 8 will provide you specific guidance on how to address this question more strategically.)

7) How will I know if I succeed and achieve my goal? As I mentioned in the beginning of this book, Stephen Covey said, "Start with the end in mind." If I can see the outcome of my work and the outcome is a good one, I am motivated by this

vision of my success. In the case of the first edition of this book, I could see the book being advertised and sold on Amazon. I could see many thousands of people benefiting from the principles in the book. And, I could see my work becoming more efficient and effective because my clients and students could readily refer to the principles we discuss in session and in the classroom.

The second of the six questions that I ask myself before embarking on a goal, "What do I plan to accomplish?" also relates to the type of goal I plan to set. There are many different types of goals, including BE, KNOW, FEEL, DO, and ACQUIRE GOALS. For example, you can set 1) BE GOALS, to become more confident, self-disciplined, patient, trustworthy, or assertive; 2) KNOW GOALS, to learn more about your spouse, automobiles, a profession, or cooking; 3) DO GOALS, to accomplish something like finishing a gardening project, losing weight, or exercising four times per week; 4) FEEL GOALS, to feel differently (less angry or more committed) about someone or something like your job, your spouse, your living circumstances, or a wayward child; and 5) ACQUIRE GOALS, to get something you want that you don't currently have like a new car, a home, an honor at work, a big screen television, or a boat. Once again, the guidance under this competency should relate back to one of the elements in your RPVS.

A good way to start the process of thinking about the types of goals you should set here (most are "BE GOALS") is to answer the following questions in terms of how they relate to each element of your RPVS. As you answer each question, you will begin to see what you need to do differently (more or less of) to make your RPVS a reality. These questions are:

- What do I need to think more about to make this element in my RPVS a reality?

- What do I need to think less about to make this element in my RPVS a reality?

- What do I need to do more of to make this element in my RPVS a reality?

- What do I need to do less of to make this element in my RPVS a reality?

- Where do I need to spend more time to make this element in my RPVS a reality?

- Where do I need to spend less time to make this element in my RPVS a reality?

- Who should I spend more time with to make this element in my RPVS a reality?

- Who should I spend less time with to make this element in my RPVS a reality?

- What will prevent me from thinking and doing the things required to make this element in my RPVS a reality?

Once again, because the purpose of the guidance under this competency is to help you begin to implement your RPVS by guiding you through the process of setting a single goal for each RPVS element. The goals you set will help you become someone different than you currently are by helping you re-engineer how you see yourself and your future. The reasoning behind this idea is the fact that you simply can't do certain things in life unless you become the kind of person who does those kinds of things.

During my last visit to China in 2011, I made several presentations on a book my wife and I published in 2001 that had to do with character education. One of the speakers who was also invited by the Chinese to speak at the same events was Dr. Stan Weed. I was fascinated by Dr. Weed's work and the character and skill traits he recommended that Chinese schools and parents teach their children. I have included these traits below as an example of some of the BE GOALS you may consider as you formulate a goal for each element in your RPVS. These are as follows:

I want to BE someone who is committed to **Worth and Potential** in all people. In this case, worth means that everyone is important and has value. Potential means having unique capacities and abilities that we can develop.

- I want to BE someone who is committed to the **Rights and Responsibilities** of all people, with the understanding that 1) rights are what all people are given at birth (choices and opportunities) or earn by working hard; and 2) a responsibility is a duty, especially the duty to make good choices. Rights are inseparable from responsibilities and can be lost when we make bad choices or violate the rights of others.

- I want to BE someone who is committed to **Fairness and Justice**, meaning that I act toward others without bias or prejudice and respect the rights, worth, and potential of others. It also means seeking solutions to problems that are objective and impartial, ensuring that consequences are appropriate for the behavior.

- I want to BE someone who is committed to **Care and Consideration**. This means I will show kindness and empathy in my actions. It requires personal acceptance of the basic principle of inherent worth and potential and giving full regard to the rights and worth of others.

- I want to BE someone who is committed to **Effort and Excellence.** This means I will work hard and persevere until a task is completed. It means not giving up because it is difficult and striving to achieve the best possible quality.

- I want to BE someone who is committed to **Social Responsibility**. This means I will make choices and take actions that will have a positive effect on other people and our world, both now and in the future.

- I want to BE someone who has **Personal Integrity**. This means I will have an uncompromising adherence to standards of ethical behavior regardless of external pressures. This means doing the right thing no matter what others do or say.

- I want to BE someone who has **Self-Control**. This means I will be able to stop, think, and make good decisions.

- I want to BE someone who exercises **Delay of Gratification**. This means I will be able to wait for the things that I want while respecting the fact that attaining many of the best things in life requires effort, time, and patience.

- I want to BE someone who has **Persistence**. This is the ability to keep trying, even when things don't go the way we would like them to. It means not giving up when the task is difficult. Persistence recognizes small successes.

- I want to BE a **Critical Thinker**. This means that I will learn to look beyond the surface, find real meaning, and weigh the pros and cons of an event or issue.

- I want to BE someone who is **Resistant to Peer Pressure**. This is the influence others have on me. It can be positive, negative, or both. Coping with Peer Pressure means I will be able to weigh what others think and feel against my own standards. It means having the courage to act according to my own convictions, regardless of what others do or say.

- I want to BE someone who can effectively engage in **Conflict Resolution**. This means that I will be able to solve problems that come up through communicating, negotiating, and/or compromising.

- I want to BE someone who can **Prioritize Competing Standards**. This means I will be able to make the better choice when two ethical choices are in conflict.

- I want to BE someone who **Sets and Achieves Worthy Goals**. In this case, I can plan and prepare for my future by setting out a meaningful and measurable path that I will follow.

My fascination with the above BE GOALS is partly due to the work of "happiness researchers" Dr. Ed Deiner and Dr. Martin Seligman, who both agree that character and skill traits are important predictors of happiness. The other and, perhaps more important, reason is that it's completely irrational to assume that someone who does not have basic character and value traits, such as respect for others' rights, self-discipline, delayed gratification, and persistence, can be happy and serene in our modern society. You can test this idea for yourself by completing the following assignment.

Although BE goals are important, you will recall that your RPVS is more than becoming, it also has to do with your desires and aspirations to learn, do, and acquire things. This means, as was mentioned in Contingency 5, that you will also need to set goals that represent what you want to do, feel, think, own, associate with, and impact by some date in the future. To help stimulate the kind of thinking you need to engage in to formulate different types of goals, you can ask yourself some of the following questions:

- How would I like things to be different in my life?

- If a miracle occurred and everything in my life was the way I think it should be, what would be different?

- What do I want to achieve in life that I have not yet achieved?

- What do I want more of?

- What do I want less of?

- What will be different and by when?

Some sample generic goals that relate to how you might respond to these questions include the following: to develop better self-esteem and self-understanding; to feel better about myself or others; to be/feel more "balanced"; to "get better" at something; to unlearn old habits (or substitute new habits or old ones); to learn how to communicate better with others (on the job and in relationships); to learn how to set and achieve goals; to control my appetite; to learn not to lay blame elsewhere—or to learn to be more responsible myself; to overcome or solve a particular problem, and/or to forgive or forget—or both; to stop acting out fears and needs with others; to overcome depression or anxiety or uncontrolled anger, etc.

Are You Ready to Achieve Your Goals?

There is a saying, "You must be, before you can do." This means if you plan to do certain things, you must become the kind of person who does those kinds of things. With this in mind, it's necessary for you to carefully determine what you need to think and do to realize your vision and achieve your goals. It will also help you evaluate your readiness to change.

The ability to achieve any goal requires 1) believing you are someone who can achieve the goal and 2) actually being someone who has what it takes to achieve the goal. Both of these conditions are necessary. However, neither of these conditions, believing or having what it takes to achieve a particular goal, independent of the other is sufficient to achieving the goal. They are only sufficient when they are taken together.

In other words, you must believe, but believing alone is not enough to achieve. To achieve you must both believe and have what is required to achieve. This is because believing something is true does not make it true. It makes it possible, but not true. Something is true only when it's rational. And something is rational only when it's based on fact. In other words, only when it's based on fact is something actually true. This means if you believe you can do something that you can actually do, your belief is true. On the other hand, if you believe you can do something that you can't actually do, it's a fact that you believe in something that is not true. In keeping with this logic, before you can expect to achieve any goal, you must 1) believe you can achieve the goal and 2) actually be able to achieve it.

With all of this in mind, in addition to helping you set goals, this competency will help you decide 1) whether or not you believe and have what it takes to accomplish these things, and 2) in the case where you do not believe or have what it takes to achieve your goals, begin the process of determining what you need to think or do differently to make up for these deficiencies.

IDEAS FOR MASTERING THIS COMPETENCY

The purposes of this competency-relevant guidance are to help you 1) begin to operationalize (or implement) your RPVS by guiding you through the process of setting a single goal for each RPVS element, 2) evaluate the rationality of your goals, and 3) start determining whether or not you are ready to achieve the goals you plan to set. Although the part of this guidance that involves assessing your readiness is somewhat redundant and may seem like "overkill," it's not. Taking a very close look at a goal before you set and start working toward the goal is key to achieving the goal. In fact, I am of the opinion that you should never set a goal that you don't plan to achieve. This process will help you decide whether the goals you set are ones that you really want to do what it takes to achieve.

1. Use the "RPVS Goal Guide" to write down at least one goal for each element in your RPVS. Be precise and only include goals that you are committed to and are confident that you can attain. For ideas about the type, content, and format of each goal, refer to the "Six Questions for Writing Goals" at the beginning of this competency and the questions relating to what you need to think or do more or less of to realize your RPVS.

2. For each goal you set using the "RPVS Goal Guide," ask the following questions:

   A. Do I believe I can achieve this goal?

   B. Do I have what it takes to achieve the goal, e.g., knowledge, skills, resources, support?

   C. Based on my responses to the last question, what do I need to think or do to get what I need to accomplish each goal?

3. To assess and begin building your motivation to achieve each goal ask yourself these questions:

   • Why do I want to achieve this particular goal?

   • What good things may happen if I achieve this goal?

   • What bad things may happen if I don't reach this goal?

   • How will things be different if I achieve this goal?

4.

(a) To further assess your readiness, including how committed you are, how confident you are, and how prepared you are, you can and ask yourself the following questions for each goal:

   • How committed am I to achieve this goal (circle number)?

   • (not committed) **0 — 1 — 2 — 3 — 4 — 5 — 6 — 7 — 8 — 9 —10** (totally committed)

   • How confident am I that I can achieve this goal (circle number)?

- (no confidence) **0 — 1 — 2 — 3 — 4 — 5 — 6 — 7 — 8 — 9 —10** (totally confident)

- How prepared am I to achieve this goal (circle number)?

- (no preparation) **0 — 1 — 2 — 3 — 4 — 5 — 6 — 7 — 8 — 9 —10** (totally prepared)

(b) Ask yourself this question: What do I need to raise each number I circled to a 10?

5. Ask this final question: What else do I need to achieve the goal (changed self-image, knowledge, skills, social support, money)?

My Plan for Mastering Competency 6

What are my short-, medium-, and long-term goals?

Competency 7
Determine What will Motivate You to Change and Grow

One of my clients who was resisting the need to change some behaviors that were interfering with his marriage and work once said to me in a therapy session, "I probably won't change until the problem gets bigger than the solution." I said "Yes, that's the way many addicts think things must play out; however, there is another option which is to make the solution bigger and better than the problem." In other words, you can hold on to a bad habit until things get so unbearable that you must change, or you can create another form of motivation that does not involve so much unnecessary suffering. For example, you can wait to experience the pain of quitting smoking until you get the diagnosis of lung cancer, which inevitably results in great pain, or you can motivate yourself to go through the pain of quitting before your health fails.

Competency 7 will help you understand the principle of motivation and how you can use different motivation techniques to increase your desire to start and persist in activities that you would not normally engage in.

First, motivation is defined as an internal drive that activates and maintains goal-oriented behaviors. It involves internal and external forces that cause us to act, whether it's eating to satisfy hunger, exercising to lose weight, going to college to improve the chances of getting a good job, or reading a book to gain additional knowledge.

Motivation has three major components. These include activation, persistence, and intensity.

Activation involves the decision to initiate a behavior like exercise. This could entail deciding to jog at a local park for thirty minutes, four days per week.

Persistence is the ongoing effort toward a goal even though obstacles such as time, energy, and resources may exist. For example, if the weather turned bad for an extended period of time and prevented you from jogging at the park, your persistence would lead you to join a fitness center to run on a treadmill, even though this may require investing in a gym membership.

Intensity is the necessary focus and consistency that goes into pursuing a goal. Whereas one person who sets the goal to jog at the park may walk instead, another person may strive to improve the time it takes to complete the jog by increasing the pace of the run.

The factors that most often diminish motivation are the lack of confidence, focus, and direction. As you will discover, several of the resiliency competencies in Section IV inherently attack these motivation killers by helping you believe you can succeed, determine specifically what you want, and provide direction toward your end goals, respectively.

The previous competency, where you both set and analyzed goals, was also designed to help you build motivation by asking you to 1) identify and visualize the benefits (positive outcomes) you expect to gain from making this change and the negative outcomes you could face if you don't reach your goals. As you may have noticed, this simple exercise has proven to be effective in building motivation to remain focused on what you want to accomplish.

Another important consideration in building and sustaining motivation is to make sure that your thoughts are congruent with your goals. To this end, the guidance under Competency 11 will teach you how to monitor and master you internal monologue in a way that ensures that your thoughts are congruent with and supportive of what you are trying to accomplish. For obvious reasons, specific positive self-statements will help strengthen your motivation to persist.

Understanding and Applying Extrinsic Motivation

Motivation is often described as being either intrinsic or extrinsic. Intrinsic motivations are those that arise from within yourself. It's the desire to do something because it's enjoyable, like reading a book or watching television or going to a movie because you enjoy the experience. My daughter in-law and son enjoys watching cooking demonstrations on television because they enjoy cooking together. I like to ride young horses for the sake of the challenge. My wife is intrinsically motivated to shop for items that can improve the appearance of our home. Again, intrinsic motivation comes from within because you want to do a good job at something because it's something that you want for yourself. That is, if you are intrinsically motivated, the enjoyment you experience would be sufficient for you to want to perform the activity in the future.

A person who is intrinsically motivated may volunteer to provide service to needy persons in the community because it makes him or her feel good to make a difference. At the same time, another person may join in the same cause because he or she believes it will make him or her look good in the eyes of others in the community. The second example is one of extrinsic motivation.

Extrinsic motivations are those that arise from outside yourself. This type of motivation reflects a desire to do something because of external rewards. Individuals who are extrinsically motivated often engage in activities that they don't enjoy because they believe they somehow will be rewarded for their efforts. In other words, it's the desire to do act because there is something in it for you, whether with or without a feeling of accomplishment. For example, a person who works at a job that she dislikes to earn more money than a lesser paying job that she enjoys is extrinsically motivated.

Another example of a individual who is extrinsically motivated is a person who decides to major in something he doesn't enjoy in college, like medicine or law, simply because he can earn more money and gain more prestige than if he had majored in a subject that he enjoyed but that may be less lucrative.

The reason for making the distinction between the two types of motivation is because they can be applied in different ways to increase activation, persistence, and intensity toward a specific goal. Because external motivation is easier to manufacture than intrinsic motivation, this competency focuses on how to create extrinsic motivation around your goals using what researchers refer to as the "Premack Principle" (Premack, 1965). This principle is based on the idea that any high probability behavior (things you really like to do) can be used to reinforce a low-probability behavior (things you don't like to do).

The Premack Principle has a number of practical advantages that can help you motivate yourself. For example, if you want to motivate yourself to do something you are not likely to do (a low probability behavior), like exercise every morning before work, you must make performing a high probability behavior like going out with friends or taking a vacation contingent (dependent) upon the low probability. That is, "Yes, I will give myself to take a quick trip to the Bahamas next month if I first [the contingency] get up and exercise before work for an hour at least four days a week for the entire month of January."

In psychological literature, the Premack Principle is applied in a motivational learning theory called Operant Conditioning. This theory relies on the principles of contingency, reinforcement, and shaping in the process of motivating compliance with desired actions.

The principle of contingency suggests that, as is implied by the above example, you are more likely to carry through on a goal and a plan of action when the things you like to do are dependent (contingent) upon the performance of things you don't necessarily like or enjoy doing. For example: "Hey self, you may NOT hang out with friends this weekend unless you work out for at least one hour before work on Monday, Tuesday, Thursday and Friday [a low probability behavior]."

On a day-to-day basis, many consequences are contingent upon behavior. For example, getting paid is contingent upon working, physical alertness is contingent upon the amount of rest you get, knowledge is dependent upon the amount of training and experience a person has, and so on. The concept of contingency is important here because it is used in connection with reinforcement (Cautela & Kastenbaum, 1995; Cole, Friedman & Bagwell, 1986) to motivate the performance of assigned duties.

Reinforcement is a principle that refers to the presentation of an event or stimuli, which, in turn, results in an increase in the frequency of a desired behavior. There are two types of reinforcement: positive and negative.

A positive reinforcer is distinguished by its specific effect on the desired behavior. If you give yourself a reinforcer—like a trip to the Bahamas—in connection with a behavior you don't necessary want to engage in—exercising before work—and your exercise behavior increases, then the trip is a positive reinforcer. Hence, the defining characteristic of a positive reinforcer is its ability to increase the desired behavior it follows, like exercising more or eating less.

The term "reward" is often used synonymously with positive reinforcers, because it is commonly understood. However, in the strictest sense, a reward is not a positive reinforcer unless it actually increases the frequency of a desired behavior. If, for example, you reward yourself with money for exercising and you don't exercise as planned, the monetary reward was not a positive reinforcer.

Some examples of reinforcers I have used to successfully increase desired behaviors include buy a new CD or book; indulge myself in watching a movie; spend an hour riding my horse; get a massage; take a walk with my wife in the park; take a day off work; listen to some of my favorite music; take a nap; take a day off from one of my goal activities; or invite friends over for a small gathering.

The principle of positive reinforcement carries a strong message: if I can identify and implement positive reinforcers, I can motivate myself to perform desired, low-probability behaviors. And the stronger the reinforcer, the more motivated I will become. Therefore, the key to motivating myself is to identify and apply strong reinforcers.

Once you have identified your individual reinforcers, it becomes possible to use them as a basis for motivating yourself toward specific goals. Formulating a reinforcement schedule that is designed to apply these principles can help with this process.

A reinforcement schedule can either be continuous or intermittent in nature. Continuous reinforcement requires reinforcing an event every time it occurs. In contrast, intermittent reinforcement requires reinforcing only after you have done something once. For example, giving yourself a reinforcer every time you work on your goals is a continuous reinforcement; but reinforcing yourself once per week, after you have met all of your goals every day of the week (the contingency), is an intermittent reinforcer.

In most instances, continuous and intermittent reinforcement schedules produce important differences in the performance of desired behavior. For example, during the initial stages of engaging in a new behavior, continuous reinforcement is more likely to motivate early performance.

Many times, a desired behavior cannot be motivated by reinforcing a single response. This is due to a number of factors, such as the complexity of the behavior, the intensity of the behavior, and the duration of the goal. In such instances, I suggest the use of another operant conditioning principle called "shaping."

Shaping a desired behavior involves reinforcing small steps or approximations toward a desired action rather than reinforcing only the desired response. The final desired behavior is eventually achieved through the reinforcement of successful approximations, which resemble the final response. For example, if you plan to lose 50 pounds over twelve months, you may want to reward yourself in stages in terms of number of pounds lost (reinforcing the loss of the first ten pounds), or for faithful adherence to a particular weight loss approach (eating less than 20 grams of fat per day for a week), or consistently following a planned exercise routine for a set amount of time (exercise for 3o minutes per day, five days per week, for two weeks). In this case you are setting up a contingency schedule that reinforces loss of the first ten pounds, eating less than 20 grams of fat per day for a week, and exercising faithfully for two weeks. This is an example of shaping, which involves setting small goals that are an approximation of and that lead to the end goal—losing 5o pounds in a year.

Once again, all of the competencies outlined in this section are inherently designed to help build motivation. The plan for building motivation outlined under Competency 7 is designed to help you systematically manufacture extrinsic motivation using operant conditioning. This is outlined in the following implementation plan.

IDEAS FOR MASTERING THIS COMPETENCY

1. List and spend some time visualizing the benefits (positive outcomes) you expect to gain from making this change. How will these benefits motivate you and help you to remain focused on what you want to accomplish?

2. List and spend time visualizing the negative outcomes you could face if you do not make this change. How will these negative consequences motivate you and help you to remain focused on what you do want to accomplish?

3. Make a list of positive reinforcers. Choose things other than food and alcohol that you will reward yourself with if you do what you plan to do.

4. Use the "CCS Reinforcement Guide" in Table 11 to develop a plan to reinforce the goals or activities you plan to work on that you know you will have difficulty motivating yourself to do without applying an extrinsic reward. In Column 1, list the goals you plan to reinforce. In Column 2, list subgoals or activities that will help you achieve the goal in Column 1. Finally, in Column 3, list the specific reinforcer that is contingent upon doing the things you listed in Column 2.

5. Evaluate your progress. If you are not doing what you plan to do, the things you have designated as reinforcers are not reinforcing. Remember, the defining characteristic of a reinforcer is that it increases the behavior it is contingent upon.

Table 11
CCS Reinforcement Guide

What Are the Goals I Plan to Reinforce?	What is the SubGoal or Goal-Related Activity I Plan to Reinforce	What is the Reinforcer? How and When Will I Reinforce My Success?

My Plan for Mastering Competency 7
What will motivate me to achieve my goals?

Competency 8
Identify and Anticipate Triggers and Barriers to Change and Growth

In addition to helping you think about and set goals, Competency 7 was also designed to help you start thinking about the barriers to achieving a goal, including lack of motivation, confidence, preparation, etc. Competency 8 will define in more detail both triggers and barriers and explain how they can undermine your ability to realize your Rational Personal Vision Statement (RPVS) and reach your goals.

Although there are innumerable triggers and barriers, the point here is that, with training and practice, you can readily identify, anticipate, and rationally cope with triggers and overcome barriers. With this in mind, the guidance under this competency will help you 1) understand what triggers are and their role in irrational thoughts and behaviors; 2) think about and prepare to avoid or respond more rationally to the triggers that have caused you problems in the past; and 3) identify, anticipate, and prepare to overcome barriers that may prevent you from making progress toward realizing your RPVS and achieving your goals.

Behavioral Triggers: What They Are and Why They Are Important

Every individual has triggers that are unique to his or her own circumstances. Irrational triggers are those things that lead to thoughts, feelings, and a chain of undesired behaviors. Fortunately, triggers can be identified, anticipated, and controlled. The competency guidance here offers a "recognize-avoid-cope" approach commonly used in cognitive behavioral therapy, which will help you recognize and change irrational thinking patterns and reactions. It also provides a step-by-step process that will help you uncover the type and nature of your triggers and to make a plan for handling them. With time, and by practicing new responses, you'll find that your unwanted triggers will lose strength, and you'll gain confidence in your ability to counter irrational triggers, urges, thoughts, physical sensations, or emotions that tempt you to think or act against your self-interest.

Recognize two types of triggers

Anything that sets off a chain reaction of predictable behaviors can be considered either a rational or irrational trigger. "Rational triggers" are people, places, and things that prompt you to think and action in ways that strengthen your commitment to health, happiness, and serenity (or well-being). Conversely, anything that causes a chain reaction resulting in irrational thoughts or actions is an "irrational trigger."

Triggers can be labeled as external or internal. "External triggers" are people, places, things, or times of day that offer opportunities or remind you of a behavior you are trying to overcome—like smoking, overeating, or drug abuse. These high-risk situations are more obvious, predictable, and avoidable than internal triggers.

Because it's easier to avoid than it is to cope with a trigger, the best initial strategy for dealing with external triggers is to avoid people, places, and things that typically trigger urges and irrational thoughts and actions that are incongruent with your goals. After you have become more competent in your ability to identify and rationally deal with triggers, you may decide to ease gradually into some situations you now choose to avoid.

"Internal triggers" can be puzzling because the urge to think or act irrationally seems to just "pop up." However, if you develop the knowledge and skills required to pause and think about it when it happens, you will be able to identify some ingrained beliefs that come out of living with, and being raised by irrational caretakers, being schooled by irrational teachers, and/or buying in to irrational ideas propagated by politicians or marketers or certain religious leaders or television programming.

The fact is, because we don't live in a perfectly rational society, all of us have been socialized in a way that has caused us, at one time or another, to embrace false beliefs that can trigger irrational thoughts, urges, emotional pain and frustration. In recognition of this fact, behavioral scientists have identified, classified, and labeled these internal triggers with various names including irrational beliefs, Cognitive Distortions, and Thought Viruses.

Irrational Beliefs as Triggers and Barriers

Albert Ellis, the father of Rational Emotive Behavioral Therapy, has studied and identified 11 common beliefs that trigger irrational thoughts that consistently undermine happiness and serenity. He labels these Irrational Beliefs. They include the following: 1) It is a dire necessity for me to be loved or approved by almost all others who are significant to me; 2) I must be thoroughly competent, adequate, and achieving, in all important respects, in order to be worthwhile; 3) The world must be fair. People must act fairly and considerately and if they don't, they are bad, wicked, villainous, or incredibly stupid; they should be severely blamed and punished; 4) It is awful and terrible when things are not the way I very much want them to be; 5)

There isn't much I can do about my anxiety, anger, depression, or unhappiness because my feelings are caused by what happens to me; 6) If something is dangerous or dreadful, I should be constantly and excessively upset about it and should dwell on the possibility of it occurring; 7) It is easier to avoid and to put off facing life's difficulties and responsibilities than face them; 8) I'm quite dependent on others and need someone stronger than myself to rely upon; I can't run my own life; 9) My past history mainly causes my present feelings and behavior; things from my past, which once strongly influenced me, will always strongly influence me; 10) I must become very anxious, angry, or depressed over someone else's problems and disturbances if I care about that person, and 11) There is a right and perfect solution to almost all problems, and it is awful not to find it.

David Burns, in his popular book, Feeling Good (1980), labels these beliefs that trigger irrational thoughts, urges, and unpleasant emotions as "Cognitive

Distortions." He states that the most problematic Cognitive Distortions are 1) All or Nothing Thinking - Thinking in black and white when many legitimate alternatives exist; 2) Over-Generalization - Pretending that everything can be judged by a single occurrence or person. Trying to "tar everything with the same brush"; 3) Mental

Filter - Seeing only the bad so you lose your perspective. Not widening your focus; 4) Disqualifying the Positive - As it says, this is the way the mind justifies inner-philosophies that make you unhappy; 5) Jumping to Conclusions (a) Mind Reader Error - Assuming people think a certain thing when you have no evidence for that, and (b) Fortune-Telling Error - Assuming that a certain thing will happen when you have no evidence for that; 6) Magnification or Minimalization - Blowing things out of proportion or minimalizing the good aspects in yourself or a situation; 7) Emotional Reasoning - Taking things personally when they weren't meant that way; 8) Should Statement - Feeling things should be a certain way that you think best - and letting it get to you when they are not; 9) Labeling or Mislabeling - Labeling yourself or some-one else, rather than seeing them for the whole person they are; and 10) Personalization - Thinking that things turn bad because you yourself are bad.

Donal Lofland, in his book titled Thought Viruses: Powerful Ways to Change Your Thought Patterns and Get What You Want in Life (1998), calls beliefs that cause irrationality "Thought Viruses." In keeping with the writings of Ellis and Burns,

Lofland states that we all have "unconscious thought patterns that distort our thinking and perception of the world." He also correctly states that these thought patters "… arise out of our learned behaviors and disempowering beliefs, and they can have a crippling effect on our professional and personal lives."

My own research related to internal triggers has revealed that individuals are triggered to start thinking about stories they tell themselves. These stories, sometimes called life scripts in the psychological literature, are influenced by our experiences with the people we are influenced by during our developmental years—our parents, teachers, and others. They help us live in and make sense of the world. They are both conscious and unconscious. And, what's most important here, these stories are both rational and irrational. The good news is that you can become aware of the conscious stories, and the irrational stories can be changed to rational ones.

Table 12
Barriers to Change and Self-Improvement

Common Barriers	What IT is and What You Can Do About IT
Lack of Knowledge	If you don't know how to do what you want to do, you will struggle. Read a book, search online, or ask someone who has the knowledge about the questions you need answers to.
False Information	Myths are popular everywhere. Don't be a victim. Take the time to make sure the information you are relying on is based on truth and not someone's wild guess or a crazy tradition that serves no good purpose other than to keep people in line. To remind my clients of

Table 12
Barriers to Change and Self-Improvement

Common Barriers	What IT is and What You Can Do About IT
	this fact I tell them, "Any fool can create a myth and any fool can believe it." Check out your information before you buy into a lie that costs you more than you are willing to pay."
Fear of Asking for Help	If you are afraid to ask for help, you can ask someone to help you who is not afraid to ask for help (laugh). Or, you can do an online search, using Google or YouTube.
Belief that You Must Learn Everything from Experience	One wise person said, "Experience is dear, but a fool learns by no other way." Learning from the "collective wisdom" of those who have gone before you is a much more efficient way of learning than having to learn everything by experience. Surely, you don't have to get cancer from smoking before you understand that tobacco use is the number one leading cause of preventable death and for every person who dies prematurely, 20 people are permanently injured by smoking. And surely, you don't believe that every cancer doctor (oncologist) must be a cancer survivor before he or she can practice medicine.
Skill Deficits	If you don't have the skills required to do what you want to do, you must do what is required to gain the skills.
Procrastination	Procrastination is the act of replacing high-priority actions with tasks of lower priority. It results from a lack of self-control and the inability to accurately predict how well you will perform tomorrow given that it often involves putting off until tomorrow the things you need to do today to attain your goals. A good way to challenge and overcome this bad habit is to only set goals and record specific steps that you are willing to follow through on. This makes the case for breaking down larger goals into small approximations of a larger goal.

Table 12
Barriers to Change and Self-Improvement

Common Barriers	What IT is and What You Can Do About IT
Limited Perspective	If you have never been out of your hometown, or have never met a person who has made significant changes in life, or have been raised by parents who are pessimists, or have been taught by people without any vision, you may suffer from lack of perspective. To overcome this, take a trip to another state or country, start and complete something you have never done before, watch the discovery channels, look at the stars late at night and ponder the immensity of the universe until you begin to realize that you have possibilities far beyond what you have ever imagined. I also suggest that you read the stories about Nick and Kyle below.
Fear of Failure	I often say the best predictor of the future is the past. To overcome a past that includes failure, you must begin to create a present that will result in a past filled with success rather than failures. After all, if you succeed at something today, tomorrow you can look back at today (the past), and point to a success. This can be accomplished by setting small, achievable goals that are stepping stones to your larger objectives. After all, nothing is preventing you from setting a goal right now that you can accomplish within minutes that will, in turn, help you achieve your larger goals.

Table 12
Barriers to Change and Self-Improvement

Common Barriers	What IT is and What You Can Do About IT
Cognitive Dissonance	Cognitive dissonance (coined by Lester Festinger in 1956) is a sense of emotional discomfort when you simultaneously hold two or more conflicting cognitions: ideas, beliefs, values, or self-image. There are two types of cognitive dissonance: value-based and change-based. "Value-Based Cognitive Dissonance," which in religious terms is called "guilt," is an emotional discomfort you experience when you think or do things that are inconsistent with what you believe to be "the right thing to think or do," like disobeying one of the ten commandments if you had a Judeo-Christian upbringing, or smoking the first cigarette if you grew up believing that smoking is dangerous, or engaging in sex before marriage if you believe that it's wrong. This type of dissonance can have a significant impact on self-esteem in that those who think and behave in ways that are inconsistent with their core values may experience a corresponding decrease in self-esteem. "Change-Based Cognitive Dissonance" occurs when you think and do things that are different than things you have thought and done in the past—like starting to exercise when you have not exercised in the past, or moving from a country where you drive on the right side of the road to a country where you drive on the left side. With both types of dissonance, the greater the discrepancy between the way you think things "should be," the greater discomfort you will experience. Both forms of dissonance must be understood and dealt with when making significant changes in your life. Both kinds of cognitive dissonance serve as an internal gauge that let you know when there is a "tremor in the force." As you become more "mindful," the "Uh Oh, Feeling" (called dissonance) will help you consciously stop and ask yourself some very helpful questions. For example, when you experience dissonance you can stop and ask yourself, "Is this new thing I am thinking or doing congruent with my core beliefs?" If your answer is, "Yes," you can say to yourself, "Oh well, this uncomfortable feeling is normal and it will pass with time." On the other hand, if your answer to this question is, "No," you can do what is necessary to bring about congruence. The most "rational" way of dealing with dissonance is to help identify and address thoughts and behaviors that are inconsistent with your desired self-image, goals, and plan of action.

Table 12
Barriers to Change and Self-Improvement

Common Barriers	What IT is and What You Can Do About IT
Seeing Yourself as a Victim or Having an External Locus of Control	Viewing yourself as a victim of circumstances takes away your power to do something about the things that happen to you on a day-to-day basis. A victim mentality is a form of negative self-fulfilling prophecy. That is, if you always think you are a victim, you will continually end up being a victim of your own negativity. What's important in psychological well-being is not what happens to you, but how we deal with it. Those who believe otherwise have an external locus of control and tend to suffer considerably more than those who decide that they are in control of how they react to the things around them.
Lack of Self-Discipline	"A simple reality which is ignored at a terrible price is that most human misery can be prevented by wise and disciplined living," Victor Brown. Self-discipline is a learned skill that leads to ultimate freedom. Although most marketers and teenagers will tell you otherwise, the only people who are truly free are those who are totally self-disciplined. This is because they can get out of bed when they want to, start and finish projects, keep their wits about them under pressure, and control their temper when it needs to be controlled. Poor time management and lack of focus or commitment are all common causes of the lack of self-discipline. Every resiliency competency discussed in Section IV is designed to improve self-discipline.
No Arms or Legs	Read the Story of Nick Vujicic and Kyle Maynard below.
Inability to See or Hear	Read the Story of Helen Adams Keller.

Table 12
Barriers to Change and Self-Improvement

Common Barriers	What IT is and What You Can Do About IT
Pessimistic Friends and Family Members	Setting and achieving goals is harder to do when you hang out with friends and family that are constantly trying to get you to relapse. It's not a secret in my profession that any time a person in a family or social system tries to change, members of the system will try to keep them the same. Ironically, this is even true when alcoholics, who after years of addiction, stop drinking. At the time they quit, a spouse, who has begged them to stop and who has tolerated all kinds of insanity, will oftentimes become irate and subconsciously say and do things that are uncharacteristic and even designed to trigger their spouse's drinking behavior. The point is, for a time at least, you may need to avoid family and friends who try to either consciously or subconsciously undermine your efforts to change.
Negative Environmental Influences	The only way to eliminate temptation is to give in to it. And, sometimes it's easier to avoid than it is to resist temptation. If you are trying to overcome drinking, it's not a great idea to hang out at a bar. Similarly, if you have a pornography problem, watching sexy movies is not going to help you overcome your addiction.
Lack of Focus	Lack of focus is a barrier for many reasons. At a minimum, if you don't stay focused on where you are going, you will undoubtedly make several missteps that make the process of change more onerous than it already is. A great way to create focus is to set precise goals that clearly articulate where you are going, how you plan to get there, and when you plan to arrive.
Insufficient Desire	A lack of desire to achieve your goals can be overcome by taking the time to understand motivation and how it can be manufactured through the techniques described in Competency 7. By learning how to focus on the task at hand, nurture motivating thoughts, neutralize negative ones, and reward small steps towards your larger goal, you can create internal desires required to get yourself out of slumps and over the hump before you lose all momentum.

Table 12
Barriers to Change and Self-Improvement

Common Barriers	What IT is and What You Can Do About IT
Inability to Deal with Setbacks and Disappointment	Everyone (all people on earth) who sets and starts working toward a goal will experience setbacks. To expect otherwise is completely irrational because it ignores they way life works. In fact, in many cases it's overcoming the setbacks in life that creates the greatest sense of accomplishment. Another stumbling block that stops you from growing and succeeding in life is fear. Your fears may include fear of failure, fear of commitment, fear of rejection, fear of public speaking, or even fear of success. Your fears will make you procrastinate, find excuses, and blame something or someone.
Lack of Confidence	According to Albert Bandura, the father of social cognitive theory, the best predictor of success or failure is the existence or lack of self-efficacy. According to Bandura, self-efficacy is "the belief or confidence in one's capabilities to organize and execute the courses of action required to manage prospective situations." In other words, self-efficacy is a person's belief in his or her ability to succeed in a particular situation. By setting small, achievable goals and at the same time learning how to minimize stress and elevate mood when facing difficult or challenging tasks, you can improve your sense of self-efficacy.

Table 12
Barriers to Change and Self-Improvement

Common Barriers	What IT is and What You Can Do About IT
Self-Limiting Beliefs	Your irrational beliefs that spawn negative self-talk and irrational stories are also responsible for your doubts, fears, and pessimism. Competency 11 will help you learn to question, challenge, and replace these limiting beliefs with empowering beliefs, thoughts, and stories that enable you to change and improve.
	Self-loathing is sometimes used to make "good" excuses to not change.
	Another self-limiting belief is "That's just the way I am." This belief kills progress and ignores the fact that, with the right plan and motivation, anyone can change.
	"Terminal Uniqueness" is used to describe individuals who developed what is often referred to as "Learned Helplessness." This is another variant on "That's just the way I am," in that it turns off all motivation because you believe your problem is so special that no one on this planet—not even an army of helping professionals—can ever provide you relief. Before you buy in to this state of mental paralysis, please read the stories of Nick and Kyle below. If after reading their stories you say something like, "Of course they were very successful, they didn't have arms and legs," you can confidently diagnose yourself as someone who has learned helplessness. Obviously, if this is the case and you don't want to do anything about it, this book nor any other book or treatment will be of any assistance. That is, you should just put the book down and have a lifelong pity party. If this doesn't sound like a fun way to finish your life, read on.
Irrational Thoughts and Behaviors	Thinking and doing things that are inconsistent with or not supportive of your desired vision, goals, and plan of action will consistently undermine your progress and ultimate success. Negative self-talk is an example of irrational thinking. Several of the techniques under Competency 11 are designed to increase congruence between your thoughts and actions, and your plan of action.

Once again, all of this is to say that irrational beliefs, whether conscious or unconscious, can serve as internal triggers that cause us harm and stand as barriers to rational living. That is, they prevent us from thinking and living rationally. The good news here is that we can identify, anticipate, and counter Thought Viruses through techniques like cognitive restructuring and life script restructuring.

Barriers to Change

One wise person said, "when you focus on the barriers, you have taken your eye off the goal." No matter what goal you set, there are going to be barriers that you must overcome to reach the goal. The variations and combinations of barriers are enumerable. The important thing is to understand they exist and must be dealt with if you hope to consistently reach your goals.

Common barriers to change and self-improvement include lack of knowledge; false information; fear of asking for help; belief that you must learn everything from experience; skill deficits; lack of commitment; procrastination; limited perspective;

fear of failure; cognitive dissonance; seeing yourself as a victim or having an external locus of control; lack of self-discipline; no arms or legs; inability to see or hear; pessimistic friends or family members; denial; negative environmental influences

(like television); lack of focus; insufficient desire; inability to deal with setbacks and disappointment; absence of passionate goals; inadequate resources; lack of confidence; self-limiting beliefs like self-loathing, indecision, low self-esteem; destructive personal habits like substance abuse; regrets about the past; irrational thoughts and behaviors; negative self-talk; pressures at work and at home; and lack of support.

Several of these barriers are listed in Table 12. In Column 2 of this Table, I have provided some basic information about what the barrier is and what you can do about it.

The good news is that with time and proper planning, you can overcome almost any barrier. This is most obvious in the lives of individuals who overcome seemingly insurmountable barriers to achieve greatness. Two modern examples of individuals that who have accomplished greatness in spite of incredible barriers (both were born without arms or legs) are Nick Vujicic and Kyle Maynard.

Nick Vujicic (born December 4, 1982) was born limbless, missing both arms at shoulder level, as well as legs. Where legs are located, he has a small foot with two toes. In spite of these obvious barriers to any number of goals the average person could easily set and reach, Nick has accomplished more than most people accomplish in a lifetime. This includes obtaining a double Bachelor's degree, serving as President and CEO of a non-profit organization (Life Without Limbs), traveling around the world as a motivational speaker, publishing several books, and releasing his own music video (http://www.nickvujicic.com).

Kyle Maynard (born March 24, 1986) is a speaker, author, and ESPY award-winning mixed martial arts athlete, known for achieving all this despite being a congenital amputee. Maynard works as a speaker for the Washington Speaker's Bureau, specializing in motivational speeches. He is the author of the memoir No Excuses:

The True Story of a Congenital Amputee Who Became a Champion in Wrestling and in Life. He has been featured on talk shows including The Oprah Winfrey Show and Larry King Live.

Maynard has trained in mixed martial arts (MMA). A documentary film, A Fighting Chance, focuses on his MMA efforts. His amateur debut fight was at Auburn Fight Night at the Auburn Covered Arena in Auburn, Alabama, on April 25, 2009. He lost his first mixed martial arts fight to Bryan Fry on a unanimous 30-27 judges'

decision. Maynard received the ESPN Espy Award for Best Athlete With A Disability in 2004. He has modeled for clothing retailer Abercrombie & Fitch. Kyle Maynard is also the owner of No Excuses CrossFit gym located in Suwanee, GA. On 15 Jan 2012, Maynard became the first quadruple amputee to climb Mount Kilimanjaro without assistance, by crawling all 19,340 feet (http://kyle-maynard.com).

The lives of Vujicic and Maynard are proof positive that, with the right approach and attitude, any barrier can be overcome. This is not to say that everything is possible. Obviously, everyone has real limitations. For example, I will never be the quarterback of the Atlanta Falcons unless I buy the team. I can, however, write and publish several books in spite of the fact that I struggled in junior high and high school because of a learning disability.

How "Ignorance" About "The Psychology of Change" Can Function as a Barrier

Although many barriers will be placed in front of you by circumstances outside your control, such as what happened to Nick and Kyle, many barriers are self-inflicted by lack of knowledge. This type of barrier can readily be overcome by dipping into the vast pool of knowledge that is now available about what does and does not work in the realm of self-improvement. A case in point is the information that was recently published by the Persuasive Technology Lab at Stanford. This prestigious group published a paper on the "Top 10 Mistakes in Behavior Change." In the context of this step, I believe that Stanford's findings serve as a good example of the barriers that being uninformed can present those who earnestly want to change. Accordingly,

I strongly recommend that you consider these mistakes as you are developing your plan of action as a part of mastering the next competency.

1. Relying strictly on willpower for long-term change: Several of the resiliency competencies address this mistake by helping you change the way you see yourself. If you start seeing yourself doing the thing you want to do, you will need considerably less willpower to do it. It will become your passion and purpose. Imagine willpower is like stretching a rubber band as far as you can and holding it there for as long as you can. Eventually, because of the stress, you are going to tire and let go, and the rubber band will snap back to the way it was. If you begin to see yourself as the kind of person who does the kinds of things you want to do, you will naturally snap back to this new vision of yourself when you are under pressure.

2. Attempting big leaps instead of baby steps: As you will see in the next competency guidance, the secret to reaching bigger goals is to set smaller, measurable steps that are approximations of the primary goal. In other words, taking tiny bites is always the best way to eat an elephant. It allows you to experience small successes, one after another.

3. Ignoring how often environment shapes behaviors: This is to say you can change your life by changing your context. Marketers understand this and always strive to make the desired behavior (purchasing their product), the easy, fun, and popular behavior. If you make your plan seem fun and easy, it will no doubt be more popular on those days that you struggle to remember why you are trying to change.

4. Trying to stop old behaviors instead of creating new ones. The point here is to focus on action, not avoidance. For the most part, all of the resiliency competencies are action-oriented in that they cause you to focus on identifying, anticipating, and replacing irrational beliefs, thoughts, and actions that can serve as triggers and barriers to success.

5. Blaming failures on lack of motivation: Again, it's hard to be motivated to do something that is very different and much harder than what you are accustomed to doing. Make the behavior fun and easier to do.

6. Underestimating the power of triggers: It's rare that a behavior ever happens without a trigger. Keep track of what you're doing; look for patterns. Find and consciously exploit triggers for good behaviors, and do what you can to eliminate the ones that cause you problems.

7. Believing that information leads to action: Humans aren't this rational. If this were the case, nurses would not smoke, financially strapped people would not play the lottery, no one who has had a heart attack would eat fatty foods, and everyone who knows anything about healthy behaviors would exercise on a regular basis.

8. Focusing on abstract goals more than concrete behaviors: This goes back to the point about the need for goals to be precise. Goals need to be specific. Generally speaking, a concrete goal is something you can do, now.

9. Seeking to change a behavior forever, not for a short time: Without a doubt, a fixed period of behavior works better than "for time and all eternity."

10. Assuming that behavior change is difficult: Behavior change is not so hard when you have the right process. Simply put, the tools under each one of the competencies discussed here and the self-directed change process introduced in Section V, if understood and applied correctly, work. Behavior change really is usually the easy part once you have a goal that is aligned with your self-image. This is because your self-image will dictate where you must go to be

OK. This is the reason I have placed so much emphasis on getting your self-image right before setting goals.

Taken together, the information provided here regarding triggers and barriers is designed to help you complete the following action steps. This competency will help you 1) identify, anticipate, and plan to rationally respond to irrational triggers; and

2) identify, break down, anticipate, and plan to overcome barriers that may prevent you from achieving your goals.

IDEAS FOR MASTERING THIS COMPETENCY

Use the following steps and guides to develop a plan that will help you 1) anticipate and respond rationally to your triggers and overcome your barriers to becoming your highest and best self. Use the information about triggers and barriers provided above to support you in your efforts.

Use the "Trigger Identification and Response Guide" to begin identifying and planning how you will respond to irrational triggers. In Column 1, list all the people, places, and things that, when you think about or encounter them, cause you to have the urge to think or do things that are incongruent with your vision and goals. In Column 2, record the things that are incongruent with your vision and goals that correspond to each trigger you listed in Column 1. Finally, in Column 3, list the things you can think or do "INSTEAD OF" those things you listed in Column 2. These "INSTEAD OFs" should be consistent with, and in support of, the actions you plan to take toward your vision and goals.

Table 13
Trigger Identification and Response Guide

Irrational Triggers That Cause Me To Think or Do Things that are Incongruent With My Vision and Goals	What have I typically thought and/or done in response to the triggers in Column 1 that is inconsistent with my vision and goals?	What can I think and/or do in response to the triggers in Column 1 that will be consistent with, and in support of, the actions I plan to take toward my vision and goals?

Use the "Anti-Flacting" technique to practice rational responses to your triggers. The term Flacting is created by combining the words feeling and acting and refers to reacting irrationally rather than making conscious, rational choices. (How to combat this process will be addressed in more detail in Competency 12b). As can be seen in Figure 8, once you experience a trigger, you will begin to experience an upsetting feeling that, in turn, causes an urge to react (think or act irrationally) instead of acting rationally. As is diagrammatically illustrated here, INSTEAD OF reacting, 1) breath for 20 seconds, and 2) say to yourself a) I am upset, b) this is an opportunity to become stronger (you do gain additional strength over your triggers every time you resist the temptation to act irrationally), and c) I will think or do rational things INSTEAD OF react. You have already listed some of these INSTEAD OFs in Column 3 of the Trigger Identification and Response Guide above.

Figure 8: Anti-Flacting

3.Use the "Barrier Identification and Response Guide" to begin identifying and planning how you will overcome barriers to your vision, goals, and plan of action.

In Column 1, list all the thoughts, emotions, actions, people, places, and things that may undermine your ability to realize your vision and achieve your goals. In Column 2, describe what you need to think and do to overcome each barrier you listed in Column 1.

Table 14
Barrier Identification and Response Guide

What barriers may prevent me from realizing my vision and achieving my goals?	What can I think or do to overcome the barriers I listed in Column 1?

Table 15
RPVS Trigger and Barrier Response Planner

RPSV Cue Word	List the Triggers and Barriers that I anticipate in connection with each RPVS element listed in Column 1.	What will I think and do to deal with each trigger and overcome the barriers?
Cue Word 1		
Cue Word 2		
Cue Word 3		

Table 15
RPVS Trigger and Barrier Response Planner

RPSV Cue Word	List the Triggers and Barriers that I anticipate in connection with each RPVS element listed in Column 1.	What will I think and do to deal with each trigger and overcome the barriers?
Cue Word 4		
Cue Word 5		
Cue Word 6		
Cue Word 7		
Cue Word 8		
Cue Word 9		
Cue Word 10		

Use the "RSPV Trigger and Barrier Response Planner" in Table 15 to begin identifying and planning how you will overcome barriers to each element in your Rational Self Perception Vision. In Column 1, list all your RSPV cue words you created in Competency 5. In Column 2, list the triggers and barriers that you anticipate in connection with each element list in Column 1. Finally, in Column 3, describe what you will do to deal with each trigger and overcome each barrier listed in Column 1.

My Plan for Mastering Competency 8

What are the barriers to achieving my goals?

Competency 9
Create a Plan of Action

Competency 9 will help you develop a daily action plan to achieve each of your goals. This plan will consist of a number of clearly defined steps that you will take to achieve each goal. Once you complete your Plan of Action, you can begin working toward your goals with confidence, knowing what it takes to reach your objective.

One of the wise adages that I learned early on when I was an Associate Director of the Public Health Department in Phoenix, AZ, was "If you fail to plan, you plan to fail." Because I did not want to fail, I put a considerable amount of time into planning. Once the plan was in place, I could move forward with confidence that we could eventually turn our goals into a reality. I was also confident that the plan would prevent us from overlooking details; remind my staff and me of our priorities; help us understand what we should and should not do; help us be more efficient by saving time, money, and energy; and help me hold myself and others accountable to make sure that we did what needed to be done to achieve our goals.

Just as I would not have been successful in managing staff and programs in a large health department without a plan of action, it's very unlikely that you will be successful in achieving a goal without a well-designed plan of action. In effect, your action plan will help you turn your goals (your vision and dreams) into a reality. If you follow the outline here, your plan will specify what you need to do, when you need to do it, and how often. It will also lay out the small, measurable, time-specific steps that you must take to achieve both smaller objectives and the larger goal.

Specifically, each action step in your plan should include the following information: what actions will occur; when you will take each action and, for how long, and what resources (i.e., money, support, equipment) you will need to carry out each action.

You should also have some criteria that assure that the steps in the plan and, the plan itself, are rational.

Rational steps and action plans are those that are: 1) Congruent: they are consistent with your vision and goals; 2) Complete: they include all the steps required to do everything that is needed to be done to achieve each goal; 3) Visible: your plan should be easy to access and available. It is not something you can write and then lock in your file drawers and forget about; 4) Clear: although an action plan is always a work in progress, the steps in the plan need to clearly specify what you plan to do, when you will do it, where you will do it, and how often it will be done; 5) Doable: the plan is not overly ambitious. You are confident that you can carry out each step as planned; 6) Effective: your planned actions should actually produce the results you expect them to produce; and 7) Flexible: make sure you build in some contingencies because the best laid plans can be thwarted by unexpected events. Another way of saying this is that you should hope for the best and plan for the worst.

Finally, as will be discussed at length in the last competency, it's important to keep track of what (and how well) you've done. Always keep track of what you have actually accomplished. Several questions that can help here include:

- Am I doing what I planned to do?

- Am I doing it well?

- Is what I am doing advancing me toward my goal?

IDEAS FOR MASTERING THIS COMPETENCY

Use Figure 9, the "Action Planner" to develop a realistic plan that will provide you with the steps you will take to achieve your goals and realize your vision. Do this by recording all of the RPVS elements in Column 1, and the goal(s) for each element in Column 2.

In Column 3, record the possible barriers to achieving each goal and realizing each vision element. In Column 4, list the specific action steps you will take to reach your goals and realize your vision. The action steps should be specific, realistic, measurable, and effective.

It's like everyone tells a story about themselves inside their own head. Always. All the time. That story makes you what you are. We build ourselves out of that story. Patrick Rothfuss, *in The Name of the Wind*

RPVS Elements	Goals	Barriers	Action Steps

Figure 9: Action Planner

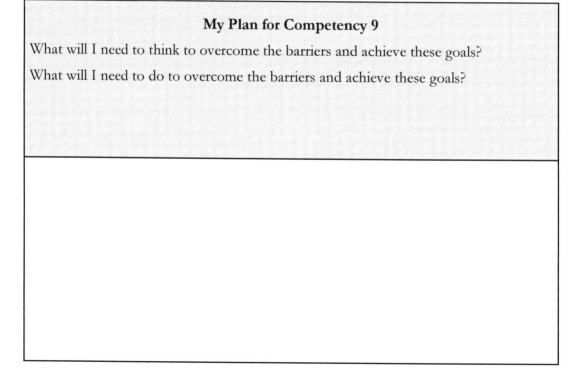

My Plan for Competency 9

What will I need to think to overcome the barriers and achieve these goals?

What will I need to do to overcome the barriers and achieve these goals?

Competency 10
Mentally Program and Internalize Your RPVS, Goals, and Plan of Action

Competency 10 explains how to use self-hypnosis and imagination to form mental images from your focused thoughts. Napoleon Hill, an advisor to President Franklin

D. Roosevelt, stated it clearly when he said, "Whatever the mind of man can conceive and believe, it can achieve." This quote is right on the mark because every creative thing anyone has ever done begins in the mind as a function of creative imagination.

As with every book I have written, study I have done, and synthetic SmartTool I have developed, the starting point for this book was in my imagination. I began the process by forming concepts, messages, ideas, and images in my creative imagination before I put a single word on paper. And, when I did start the arduous task of writing these ideas down, one of the first quotes I came across reinforced the points I will make here about the power and importance of imagination. It's a quote by Albert Einstein: "I am enough of an artist to draw freely upon my imagination. Imagination is more important than knowledge. Knowledge is limited. Imagination encircles the world."

My point here is that a necessary first step in the psychology of change or any creative process, including what goes into the process of making personal or interpersonal changes, is imagination. This means that in order for you to become more rational in your life, you must first imagine it. If you cannot imagine it in your mind, you cannot create it in reality. This is true with the way you think about yourself (your self-perception), as well as rational thoughts and actions.

Self-hypnosis, Visualization, Mental Imaging, and Rehearsal are synthetic learning techniques that rely on your creative imagination to help you improve the rationality and congruence between your self-perception, thoughts, and actions. The guidance provided in this competency will elaborate on how to use these techniques to increase your commitment and intensity toward improving your skills, achieving your goals, and realizing your vision.

To use your imagination effectively you must first realize its enormous power to visualize objects, situations, and circumstances and to respond to impulses, sound, taste, and other sensations. As a reminder of this power and how readily it can be accessed, simply close your eyes and imagine yourself standing in front of a large audience that is looking at you as you begin to give a speech about the power of imagination; or imagine yourself being chased by an angry dog, or wrestling a bear and winning, or being swallowed whole by a whale, or winning the lottery, or being pro-nounced king or queen of your country, or being asked on a date by the most attractive person you can "imagine," or standing on a tall building in a hurricane force wind, etc. The capacity to imagine is built into every person and is activated at a very young age. It is the ability to think about people, places, and things beyond your present situation. It's a fundamental aspect of the human condition that allows us to transcend our present circumstances and think about the future, remember the past, solve problems in the present, and strategize about how to effectively create and implement new ideas.

Unfortunately, many parents and educational systems don't teach students how to harness or use their imagination in productive ways such as considering new possibilities, alternatives, and hypothetical scenarios. Because of this deficiency in socializing and educating young people, many individuals go through life without taking advantage of one of the most powerful tools they have for personal and professional success that oftentimes depends on the ability to develop imaginative, innovative thinking. With this in mind, this competency guidance will help you maximize your imagination in a way that enables you to control it and visualize only what you intentionally decide to visualize and, in turn, change your life in accordance with your will and imagination.

Imagination has many positive applications, but often it is not well-developed or controlled. This lack of control can lead to lack of control over your life in general. As with the previous competencies, the guidance here will help you better control what you allow to enter your mind and how you use this information to increase your rationality.

Although much of what you have done as a part of developing the previously discussed competencies has no doubt engaged your imagination, Competency 10 outlines a process and a number of techniques you can use to begin honing and controlling your imagination in more productive ways. When using these techniques, you can increase your internal motivation and intensity toward achieving your goals with things like motivational literature, pictures, images, videos, and music that are in sync with what you are trying to accomplish. For example, by mentally creating, recreating, and focusing on a goal and the steps required to achieve this goal, and then anticipating and focusing on ways of overcoming barriers to this goal, you can acquire and amplify the personal confidence required to make permanent changes that include improving your self-perception and your ability to think and act rationally.

One thing that is different about the techniques you will learn here is that they are designed to help you focus on and address specific issues in the form of self-directed assignments. These assignments rely on the use of creative imagination to amplify your capacity to benefit from each technique because they allow you to focus on whatever unique need you have at the time. The assignments you can give yourself are only limited by your imagination, and they include such things as setting goals; sorting, prioritizing and solving problems; learning new skills; relaxing and/or remaining calm under pressure; becoming more confident; making a presentation to any size group; overcoming bad habits and addictions; answering media questions; and/or improving relationships.

IDEAS FOR MASTERING THIS COMPETENCY

The steps you will follow in using these and other techniques that you will create as you become more proficient with the process are as follows:

1. Start at conscious baseline.

2. Give yourself an assignment, with a specific objective and purpose: set and attain goals; sort, prioritize, and solve problems; learn new skills; relax and/or remain calm under pressure; become and remain confident; make a presentation to any

size group; overcome addictions; silence your inner critic; internalize your vision and goals; answer media questions; and/or improve relationships. Focus on one purpose at a time.

3. Based on the assignment you give yourself, write out suggestions to "make to yourself" as you get into your relaxed state. These suggestions should be consistent with your assignment and help you stay in the "present." For example, you should use "I am" instead of "I will be" statements.

4. Create a place in your mind where you will carry out the assignment, e.g., a workshop, practice field, or resort, decompression chamber, gymnasium, etc.

5. Select a technique that will help you achieve your purpose.

6. Close your eyes and take time to relax (breathe) until you are ready to take on the assignment.

7. Tune inward with the initial focus on a slow, relaxed breath, while at the same time imaging that you are going into a deeper state while counting down slowly from 5, 4, 3, 2, to 1.

8. At this point, focus all of your senses to work on your assignment using the suggestions you decided on related to the assignment. Once again, when making suggestions, use "I am" instead of "I will be" statements.

9. End your assignment with the belief that you are going to experience positive benefits from this experience, and you are going to become alert and come out this deeply relaxed state after counting to three: 1, 2, 3.

10. Return to your baseline.

11. Record your progress so you can carry your accomplishments and good memories with you.

The following comments will help you better understand the process outlined above. Specifically, I provide you with some relaxation techniques and some ideas regarding how to "construct" a place in your mind. I also provide you with some visualization and creativity exercises you can use to mentally program and internalize your vision, goals, and plan of action.

Relaxed Body, Relaxed Mind

As you can see from this list of steps, one of the first things you need to do with each technique is to relax. This is because a relaxed body equates with a relaxed mind, which, in turn, improves your ability to focus and attend to your self-directed visualization and imagery assignments.

Relaxation techniques typically combine breathing and focused attention to calm your body and mind. If used correctly, these techniques will help you quiet your inner critic and increase your ability to carry out your self-directed imagery assignments. In addition to amplifying the benefits of mental imagery and rehearsal, learning and applying relaxation techniques can help with a number of stress-related problems. This is documented in the U.S. National Institutes of Health, National

Center for Complementary and Alternative Medicine (NCCAM) Clinical Digest, published in December 2012, which reports evidence that relaxation techniques may be an effective intervention for treating a number of stress-related disorders, including anxiety, phobias and panic disorder; depression; headaches; lung function and asthma; immune function; heart disease and heart symptoms; hypertension; chronic insomnia; and irritable bowel syndrome. Other reliable sources have reported evidence that relaxation may help mitigate chronic pain, fibromyalgia, premenstrual syndrome, psoriasis, and hyperactivity related to ADHD. The point is, investing the time to relax before using any of the following visualization techniques may have a number of benefits beyond helping you improve your rationality related to your self-image, thoughts, and behaviors.

Selecting the Right Relaxation Technique

The right technique, in the present context, is the one that suits your personal liking and helps you relax and calm your mind in preparation for completing your self-directed imagery assignment(s). Based on my experience with clients and students, the most widely studied techniques that have direct application to this competency are deep breathing and progressive muscle relaxation. Other effective techniques include meditation, guided imagery, self-hypnosis, yoga, Tai Chi, massage, and exercise.

The steps you should follow when using deep breathing and progressive muscle relaxation as a means of getting in to a relaxed state before doing your visualization and imagery exercise are as follows:

Deep Breathing

1. Get in a comfortable position.

2. Close your eyes.

3. Breathe in through your nose and out through your mouth.

   • As you breathe in through your nose, visualize inhaling pure oxygen that is coated with relaxation.

   • As you breathe out through your mouth, exaggerate the exhalation by visualizing blowing out a birthday candle and imagining that you are releasing tension, stress, and strain. The exaggerated exhale will speed up the relaxation process.

4. Continue breathing in and out until you are able to feel a sense of calm and have quieted most of the distracting thoughts (e.g., your inner critic) that may interfere with your imagery exercise.

5. Begin your visualization exercise.

Progressive Muscle Relaxation

1. Get in a comfortable position.

2. Close your eyes.

3. Visualize scanning your body up and down to find an area that is "more" relaxed than most other places on your body.

4. See yourself breathing into that area (in through your nose and out through your mouth) while imagining that your inhalation is causing the "more" relaxed area to increase in diameter and your exhale is releasing stress.

5. Do this for about 30 seconds.

6. Now visualize yourself scanning your body to find an area that is more tense than other parts of your body. Once you have identified this area, start breathing in and out. Once again, imagine that your inhale is relaxing the area that is "more" tense than other areas in your body. Do this for about 30 seconds.

7. Now start tensing and relaxing muscle groups from your feet to your head while breathing in pure oxygen/relaxation and breathing out stress/tension/strain. For example:

   - Imagine flexing the muscles in your feet for five seconds and then releasing. The tensing of muscles will bring blood to the area where you have flexed and cause a sense of warmth and relaxation. Continue breathing in and out while continuing to imagine yourself taking in pure oxygen/relaxation and releasing stress and strain.

   - Now flex your lower legs (your calf muscles) for five seconds while repeating the breathing process.

   - Next, go to your upper legs, then buttocks, abdomen, chest and back, hands, arms, shoulders, neck, and then face. Flex each muscle area for five seconds and then release while continuing to breathe throughout the entire process. Breathe in pure oxygen/relaxation and exhale all the bad things that are causing your body to tense up and feel stress.

8. After go through the muscle groups you should be prepared to start the imagery exercise. If not, go through the process of tensing and relaxing your muscles again and again until you are feeling calm.

9. Begin the imagery exercise.

Constructing Places in Your Mind

As I mentioned above, it's helpful to construct a "place in your mind" when you are doing your visualization work. Don't worry about how many places you build as it's estimated that humans have about 100 billion brain cells. This number does not include support cells, such as glial cells, that help the neurons; these cells have been calculated to be at least ten times more numerous than neurons. This is to say, you have plenty of real estate to work with. Furthermore, don't skimp on the quality of the places you build. Your virtual mental budget is only limited by your imagination.

Once again, you can increase your commitment and intensity toward achieving your goals with things like motivational literature, pictures, images, videos, and music that are in sync with what you are trying to accomplish. With these directions in mind, I have provided you with a number of examples of "mental places" you can create and with the exercise you can carry out in these places. The place I recommend that everyone learn is called a "Mental Home Movie Theater."

Mental Home Movie Theater - Create a movie theater in your mind, including seating and a screen where you will watch yourself play out a script related to something you want to happen a certain way. Mentally write a script and play the part. Focus on the present as if you are the character you are watching on screen.

Visualize a perfect performance until it mentally happens and you are confident you can play the part in real life. These steps are:

1. Create your theater (preferably an IMAX).

2. Write a very good, very comprehensive script. Remember to write a script for each goals/element in your vision.

3. Get in a relaxed state, and then

4. Watch yourself play your part in the movie over and over again until you believe you are the character you are watching. Watch yourself reach your goals!

5. Record your progress in your journal.

Mental Practice Room or Field - Whereas the "Mental Movie" technique involves watching yourself play a part, this technique involves visualizing yourself practicing some activity like giving a speech, hitting a golf ball, calmly discussing a problem with your spouse, asking for a raise at work, eating a healthy diet, responding rationally to your common triggers, etc. Do this by:

1. Getting into a relaxed state.

2. Decide on a purpose.

3. Start Practicing.

4. Record your progress.

Problem Room - This "room" is a place in your mind where you can store your small, medium, and large problems. The rules of this technique are:

1. Place all problems in this room.

2. Decide how you will determine the size and importance of the problem.

3. Organize your problems by size and importance.

4. Set a regular schedule to visit, review, and/or work on your problems.

5. Record and store successes and failures for future reference.

Problem Cards - This exercise is one of the most effective mental strategies you can possibly use when you feel overwhelmed. It will help you get all of your problems out of your head and onto paper. The steps you will use are as follows:

1. Get 3x5 cards.

2. List each of your most pressing problems on a separate card.

3. Keep your cards with you throughout the day. Also carry a pencil or pen with you.

4. Take your cards to a virtual "problem room" two times per day. While you are in this room, review your problems for several minutes.

5. At any time you have a thought about a problem on one of your cards, write it down on the card.

6. When the problem on a card is solved, place the card in a designated drawer in your house.

Happy Place - Create a place in your mind that you can go to think about all the things that make you happy. You can also think about what you need to do more or less of to increase your happiness. Follow these steps:

1. Ask yourself the following questions to identify some things you can think or do differently to increase your happiness:

    (a) What do I need to think more about to increase my happiness?

    (b) What do I need to think less about to increase my happiness?

    (c) What do I need to do more of to increase my level of happiness?

    (d) What do I need to do less of to increase my level of happiness?

    (e) Where do I need to spend more time to increase my level of happiness?

    (f) Where do I need to spend less time to increase my level of happiness?

    (g) Whom should I spend more time with to increase my level of happiness?

    (h) Whom should I spend less time with to increase my level of happiness?

    (i) What will prevent me from thinking and doing the things required to increase my level of happiness?

2. Get into a relaxed state.

3. Go to your happy place.

4. Start visualizing yourself doing more and less of those things you wrote down in response to the questions listed above.

5. Record your progress.

Bad Memory/Failure Dungeon - This is a place where you will lock up all bad experiences and memories that cause you emotional pain. This allows you to confine all the memories that cause you pain in one place. The rules of this technique are:

1. You must schedule and record all visits.

2. You can only visit one memory at a time.

3. The purpose of each visit is to find some redeeming quality about the memory.

4. If you can't find one, you can't visit again until you come up with a redeeming quality that you can attach to the memory at your next visit.

5. You must put the memories back in prison after the visit.

6. Record your progress.

Worry World - This is a place in the mind that you can create for the purpose of scheduling and carrying out your plans to "worry like crazy!" I say "crazy" because if you think about it, worrying is crazy. Why? It doesn't work; therefore, it's not rational. In fact, constant worry is harmful in that it creates unnecessary stress. That said, if you are a worrier I strongly recommend this game. To play Worry World, do the following:

1. Make a list of all the things you want to worry about.

2. Schedule specific times to worry.

3. Set a time limit.

4. Stop and start worrying on time.

5. Worry as much as you like when you are in Worry World.

6. Do not worry at all when you are not in the World. That is, if you catch yourself worrying outside of Worry World, quickly schedule an appointment and go there. The trick is to be disciplined about never worrying unless you are in Worry World at the scheduled time.

7. Record what you learn after each session.

I Don't Understand File - This is a place in your mind where you can store away things that happen to you that you don't understand. Things happen in our lives that we don't plan and we can't explain. Instead of getting frustrated and wasting countless hours trying to understand "Why" something happens, you can file these things away in a mental "I Don't Understand" folder, file cabinet, and room. If you go through life trying to figure out why something bad happened or why things didn't work out, it will cause you to become bitter and stuck in life. Completing this exercise will allow you to move forward until you get the information you need to put these "I Don't Understand" events into a context and perspective that allows you to learn from the events rather than ruminate over them.

Before I provide you with the steps to this technique, I will tell you a story that has helped me when I don't understand something that has happened in my life. Over the years as I have travelled to different parts of the globe, I have come to realize a universal principle that is taught in the form of stories in every country I have visited. Although the stories differ, the principle is the same. One of my favorite stories can apply when you start working in your "I Don't Understand Room" is called Hakuna Matata (a Swahili phrase that can be translated literally as "There are no worries)." Although I don't know how much of it is true (and I have "tweaked" it for the purposes of making a specific point), it does make for a great story.

I heard this version of the story when I was on assignment with the World Health Organization (WHO) in Nigeria. My job was to use my skills as research psychologist in helping the Nigerian government set up a "communication surveillance system" (Cole, 2006) around an outbreak of H1N4 (bird flu). This system was designed to get information from villagers across the country about how they perceived the bird flu, what they did with a sick chicken, what they did with a dead chicken, etc. While leading a team of researchers I was responsible for meeting with the chief of a large (250,000 population) Muslim village. Normally this would not have been a problem, except for the fact that there was a civil war going on between Muslims and Christians.

Because of this, a WHO security officer provided me with some very sobering training about how to get in and out of the village safely. He also explained in some detail how I should meet and greet the Chief. When I entered the home of the Chief,

I immediately gained an appreciation for the precautions taken by the WHO security officer, given that he was surrounded by guards with machine guns. This gave me a rush of adrenaline that helped me to follow protocol to the letter. Fortunately, the

Chief turned out to be a very kind, very gracious host. After asking me to sit down for a conversation I told him my purpose for coming. In his response he used the words Hakuna Matata. When he said this, I must have looked shocked because the way he used the phrase was somewhat different than the way it was used in the Disney movie and the Broadway Musical, The Lion King, where the phrase was interpreted to mean, "Don't worry, be happy." Instead of this interpretation, the chief used the phrase to mean "It's all good," or "Whatever happens to us is for a reason."

To clarify his use of the phrase in this way, the Chief told me a story about his great grandfather, which illustrates the point I want to make here regarding the "I Don't Understand File." The Chief said his great grandfather was a King in Northern

Nigeria near the Congo. He said the King had a servant who was very faithful in carrying out his every command. The only problem was that no matter what happened, the servant would often say the words "Hakuna Matata," meaning "It's all good." Even though this was annoying to the King, he put up with it since the servant was so obedient. That is until one day, when the King and a hunting party were out hunting elephants. During this hunt the King's weapon misfired and blew off the end of one of his fingers. When his favored servant noticed the King was writhing in pain, he started trying to comfort him and in the midst of his attempts to bring some relief to the King, he used the words "Hakuna Matata." This infuriated the King so much that when they got back to the village he had his servant put in a dungeon. A few months later the King was on another hunting trip near the Congo. During the hunt the King and his hunting party were surrounded by headhunters (aka, cannibals) and taken back to their village as captives. Not long after the King and his hunting party arrived at the headhunters' village, the cannibals started sacrificing the men in the King's hunting party one by one to their pagan Gods.

Because he was dressed as royalty, the King was going to be sacrificed last. When he was being prepared for sacrifice, they noticed he was missing one of his fingers and, because it was bad juju to sacrifice anyone to their Gods who was not whole, the

King was released. As the King was walking through the jungle back to his own village, he kept looking down at his hand where his finger used to be and saying out loud the words, "Hakuna Matata." That is, he realized that his servant was right; it was a good thing that he lost his finger. With this in mind, the first thing the King did when got back to the village was to go to the dungeon and have his servant released. When the

King saw his servant he started apologizing for putting him in the dungeon. In response, the servant said, "Hakuna Matata." The King, in turn asked, "How can you say 'it's all good' that you have been in this dungeon for this long time, especially when you look so thin and pale?" The servant then said, "My dear King, had you not put me in this dungeon when you did, I would have been on this hunting trip with you and I would have been sacrificed because I am whole."

Once again, this story teaches the idea that we can choose to look at everything that happens to us as a "good thing." I know this much, when I chosen to put a positive spin on what initially appears to be a "bad" situation (even though my heart screamed otherwise), it has helped me be "more OK" when things in my life were terribly "not OK." It has also helped buy the time I needed to gain the perspective required to understand what "I could not understand" in the first place. And, I might add, in many instances the information and perspective I needed to understand things that I simply "couldn't understand" in my youth did not come until years after the unpleasant events took place.

To use the I Don't Understand File, follow these steps:

1. Create a folder, file cabinet, and room in your mind where you will keep all the things that happen to you that you "Don't Understand."

2. Schedule and record all visits to this room.

3. Only visit when you are in a good mental state.

4. When you visit, do so with the purpose of finding some redeeming quality about the event you "Don't Understand."

5. If you can't find gain any insight during the visit, carefully put the file back in its place until the next visit.

6. Record your progress.

Service Station - This is a place where you go to think about and plan ways to serve others. Based on the self-report of individuals who are truly happy and successful, this is one of the most effective techniques for increasing a sense of meaning, positive emotion, purpose, and accomplishment. The steps are as follows:

1. Create a mental room decorated with pictures and quotes that remind you of the benefits of serving others. The room should also have reminders of the kinds of service you want to provide and the types of individuals you would like to serve.

2. Visit the room on a regular basis to review your successes and failures in serving others and to make new plans to serve.

3. Record and store successes and failures for future reference.

The Armory - This is a room that you visit at the beginning of each day. This is where you begin building and implementing your action plan. Do this by following these steps:

1. Create a mental armory where you can develop a resiliency plan.

2. Go through the steps in your plan.

3. Record your progress.

Good Memory Lane - Your can create a mental place—or you can actually go to a physical place—where you can go to think about and dwell on good memories. Do this by following these steps:

1. Create a place or mental room with reminders of good memories. Include pictures, music, and other reminders of good memories. (Again, you can also create an actual place, such as a quiet room in your house or a favorite outdoor spot).

2. Get relaxed using the relaxation techniques provided earlier.

3. As you are in your mental or physical place, relish in all the good memories.

4. Record all the good things you remembered, along with the good feelings you had when you were revisiting these good memories.

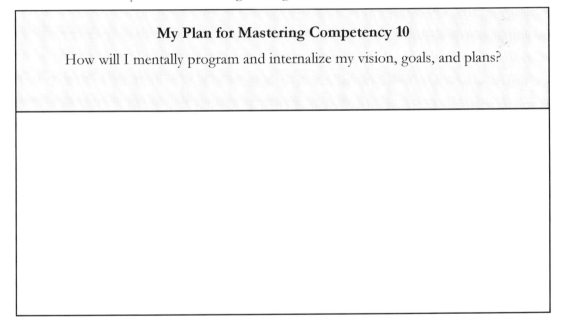

My Plan for Mastering Competency 10

How will I mentally program and internalize my vision, goals, and plans?

Competency 11
Observe and Master Your Internal Monologue

Our conscious mind has a voice. This is evident because as humans we talk to ourselves all of the time—we think about what we are thinking and feeling. In light of this well-known factor, many prominent individuals across history have testified that positive thinking is key to living a happy and successful life. Some examples of quotes from famous individuals about the importance of positive thinking are as follows:

- For as he thinks in his heart, so is he. (Proverbs 23:7)

- We are shaped by our thoughts; we become what we think. When the mind is pure, joy follows like a shadow that never leaves. (Buddha)

- Jesus said unto him, If thou canst believe, all things are possible to him that believeth. (Mark 9:23)

- Our thoughts determine our lives. (Elder Thaddeus of Vitovnica)

- Mind is the Master power that moulds and makes, and Man is Mind, and evermore he takes the tool of Thought, and, shaping what he wills, Brings forth a thousand joys, a thousand ills: He thinks in secret, and it comes to pass: Environment is but his looking-glass. (James Allen)

- The World is what we think it is. If we can change our thoughts, we can change the world. (H.M. Tomlinson)

- We become what we think about. (Earl Nightingale)

- Change your thoughts and you can change the world. (Norman Vincent Peale)

- The pessimist sees the difficulty in every opportunity; an optimist sees the opportunity in every difficulty. (Winston Churchill)

- A man is but the product of his thoughts; what he thinks, he becomes. (Mahatma Gandhi)

- Success is a state of mind. If you want success, start thinking of yourself as a success. (Dr. Joyce Brothers)

- Once you replace negative thoughts with positive ones, you'll start having positive results. (Willie Nelson)

- Every thought is a seed. If you plant crab apples, don't count on harvesting Golden Delicious. (Bill Meyer)

- Thoughts become things… Choose the good ones! (Mike Dooley)

- Cynics do not contribute, skeptics do not create, doubters do not achieve. (Gordon B. Hinckley)

Another example of how the choice to think positively or negatively has long been understood as a factor in how things work out in our lives is found in the poem titled "Thinking," by Walter Wintle.

> *If you think you are beaten, you are,*
> *If you think you dare not, you don't.*
> *If you like to win, but you think you can't,*
> *It is almost certain you won't.*
>
> *If you think you'll lose, you're lost,*
> *For out in the world we find,*
> *Success begins with a fellow's will.*
> *It's all in the state of mind.*
>
> *If you think you are outclassed, you are,*
> *You've got to think high to rise,*
> *You've got to be sure of yourself before*
> *You can ever win a prize.*
>
> *Life's battles don't always go*
> *To the stronger or faster man.*
> *But soon or late the man who wins,*
> *Is the man who thinks he can.*

Although it's true that we tend to become what we think about most of the time, behavioral scientists have demonstrated that to successfully achieve a goal requires more than positive thinking. As I explained in Section III, "positive thinking" is an oversimplification of reality; it's more accurate to label positive thinking an "additive" to rational thinking. That is, positive thinking is necessary to success and emotional well-being, but it's not sufficient. This is because positive thinking, although it serves to elevate emotions, left to itself, often is partial, uninformed, biased and/or downright prejudiced.

What's more effective than positive thinking is rational thinking. This is because rational thinking consists of beliefs and thoughts that are logical, consistent with known facts and reality, help you feel the way you want to feel, help you achieve your goals and solve your problems, and support a rational self-perspective.

Albert Ellis, the father of Rational Emotive Behavioral Therapy (REBT), once said:

> "We tend to formulate our emotions and our ideas in terms of words and sentences. These effectively become our thoughts and emotions. Therefore, if we are basically the things we tell ourselves, any type of personal change requires us to look first at our internal conversations. Do they serve us or undermine us?"

Ellis's point that we need to "look at our internal conversations" is the basis for this competency. Based on my experience in helping individuals overcome every kind of problem you can imagine, I can confidently state that before you can make and sustain change in your life, you must understand how to "see" what you think about before you can change your thought patterns. Once you learn to monitor and see your thoughts, you can then do something about them.

This competency guidance will help you systematically observe and master your internal monologues in a way that consistently ensures rational, self-directed, quality thoughts about any subject, content, or problem. You will do this by learning to observe how you think, make a connection between what you feel at anyone time and what you are thinking, evaluate your thinking in a way that helps you distinguish between irrational and rational thoughts, self-correct your thinking by discarding irrational thoughts that do not support your vision, goals, and plan of action and replace them with rational with thoughts that are supportive of your vision, goals, and plan of action.

The techniques introduced here are based on Cognitive Behavioral Therapy techniques referred to as Cognitive Restructuring (David Burns), Thought Virus Replacement (Donald Lofland, 1998), Irrational Thought Replacement (Ellis,

Harper & Powers, 1975), and Life Script Restructuring (Cole, 2014). All of these methods are designed to help identify and replace dysfunctional, or irrational, thoughts with more rational alternatives. Specifically, these techniques typically involve learning how to systematically 1) monitor thinking, especially during times of distress, 2) identify thoughts which are antecedents to negative emotions-the identified thoughts are called such things as Cognitive Distortions, Thought Viruses, or irrational thoughts, 3) challenge the validity of the identified maladaptive (or irrational) thoughts, and 4) substitute the Cognitive Distortions with more rational thoughts.

Generally speaking, Figure 10 illustrates how these techniques and, more specifically, "Irrational Thought Replacement" works. As you can see, in this figure we all have thoughts that influence how we feel (our emotions). The logic illustrated here is that if you think irrationally, you will feel upset and, in turn, act irrationally.

To overcome this maladaptive process, these techniques help you place filters on your thoughts. This means you will examine your thoughts and "throw out" the ones that may cause you to act irrationally. Each of the "rational filters" here is a different question that you will ask of your thoughts in an effort to distinguish the ones that are rational from the irrational ones. Simply put, when you learn to pay careful attention to your thoughts, you will begin to ask yourself whether or not the thoughts are rational. As depicted in Figure 10a, you can ask yourself these types of questions:

- Is this belief or thought logical?

- Is it consistent with known facts and reality?

- Will it help me feel the way I want to feel?

- Does it contribute to a Rational Self Perception (RSP)?

- Will it contribute to my sense of well-being?

- Will it help me solve my problems?

- Will it help me achieve my goals?

Figure 10a: Using "Rational Questions" to Filter Out Irrational Thoughts

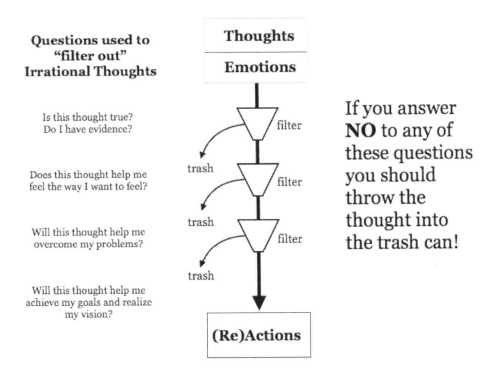

Questions used to "filter out" Irrational Thoughts

Thoughts

Emotions

Is this thought true?
Do I have evidence?

filter

trash

Does this thought help me feel the way I want to feel?

filter

trash

Will this thought help me overcome my problems?

filter

trash

Will this thought help me achieve my goals and realize my vision?

(Re)Actions

If you answer **NO** to any of these questions you should throw the thought into the trash can!

If you answer no to any of these questions, you discard the thought. Conversely, if you answer yes to all of the questions, the thought or belief is rational and will support you in your efforts to consistently think and live rationally.

While completing the exercises in Competency 11, I suggest that you refer to Albert Ellis's 11 irrational beliefs, which were introduced in Competency 8. You can find this list in the Thought Observation and Restructuring Guide: Part 1 (labeled as Reference 2), later in this competency.

As was mentioned above, the process of repeatedly monitoring, evaluating your thoughts, and discarding those that you deem to be irrational, is not all that is involved in changing maladaptive thoughts to more rational ones. Because you simply can't stop thinking, when you do discard a thought you must replace it with another thought. This process is depicted in Figure 10b. In this figure, you can see that I have provided you with a place to record the thoughts you plan to think

"INSTEAD OF" the thoughts you put in the trashcan. Once again, these INSTEAD

OFs must be rational, in that they are logical, consistent with known facts and reality, help you feel the way you want to feel, contribute to and support your vision, give you a sense of well-being, and help you solve your problems and achieve your goals.

Figure 10b: Deciding on "Rational Questions" to Filter Out & Replace Irrational Thoughts

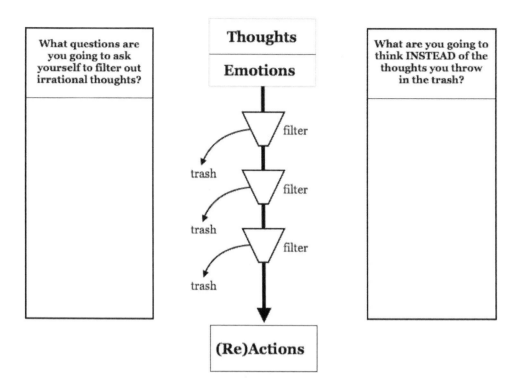

As is the case with Irrational Thought Replacement, "Cognitive Restructuring" also helps you identify and change out maladaptive thoughts. The main difference is that in the case of Cognitive Restructuring, the maladaptive or irrational thoughts are referred to as Cognitive Distortions. As was mentioned in Competency 8, David

Burns, in his popular book Feeling Good, labels these beliefs that trigger irrational thoughts, urges, and unpleasant emotions as Cognitive Distortions. To review, Burns states that the most problematic Cognitive Distortions are 1) All or Nothing Thinking, 2) Over-Generalization, 3) Mental Filter, 4) Disqualifying the Positive, 5) Jumping to Conclusions (including Mind Reader Error and Fortune-Telling Error), 6) Magnification or Minimalization, 7) Emotional Reasoning, 8) Should Statement, 9) Labeling or Mislabeling, and 10) Personalization.

You can find a more detailed description of these Cognitive Distortions in the Thought Observation and Restructuring Guide: Part 1 (labeled as Reference 3) later in this competency. (This list was first introduced in Competency 8). Once you learn to identify your own Cognitive Distortions, or irrational thoughts, you can begin the task of replacing them with rational ones.

Another technique that illustrates the process of systematically changing irrational thoughts to more rational ones is called "Thought Virus Replacement." As with the other techniques I just described, this approach is another Cognitive Reappraisal

Technique that draws upon many of the same principles that Cognitive Behavioral Therapy and Rational Emotive Behavioral Therapy are based upon. What's different here is my use of the term "Thought Virus" (coined by Donald Lofland in his book Thought Viruses: Powerful Ways to Change Your Thought Patterns and Get What

You Want in Life) in place of the terms "Irrational Thoughts" or "Cognitive Distortions."

I like to refer to maladaptive thoughts as Thought Viruses for two reasons: 1) I have worked for the US Centers for Disease Control and Prevention for 22 years, and during that time I have learned a lot about pathogens, including viruses, and more importantly, 2) talking about Thought Viruses is easier to understand and explain than a Cognitive Distortion." Even though the term "Cognitive Distortion" sounds more scientific, it is simply a label given to thoughts that cause problems. That said,

I define a Thought Virus the same way I define irrational thoughts and Cognitive Distortions. In other words, a Thought Virus is any belief or thought that is not logical or true, does not contribute to a Rational Self Perception (RSP), does not improve a sense of well-being, will not help you solve your problems, and will not help you achieve your goals.

Once again, as with "Irrational Thought Replacement" and "Cognitive Restructuring," the objective of this "Thought Virus Replacement" technique" is to help you learn to systematically identify and replace maladaptive thoughts.

I have provided some examples of the Thought Virus Replacement technique in Figure 11. This figure shows Thought Virus and "Remedies" to each virus. In this metaphor, the remedies are simply replacement thoughts that you can use to counter Thought Viruses. These new thought remedies are thoughts you will plan to think INSTEAD OF the beliefs and thoughts that are labeled Thought Viruses.

Accordingly, they should correspond with and logically replace the Thought Virus you are struggling with.

As you can see in this figure, the process of replacing Thought Viruses involves listing thoughts that make you upset in column 1, and listing corresponding thoughts that you plan to think "INSTEAD OF" each Thought Virus in Column 2. Once again, this is exactly the same logic as Cognitive Restructuring and Irrational Thought Replacement where, in both instances, you learn to identify, filter out, and replace maladaptive thoughts with thoughts that are logical and consistent with known facts and reality, help you feel the way you want to feel, contribute to a Rational Self Perception, improve a sense of well-being, solve your problems, and achieve your goals.

When I teach the Thought Virus Replacement technique, I typically expand on the Thought Virus metaphor by making the point that irrationality, or irrational thoughts and actions, are the primary cause of emotional upset and instability. This means that anyone or anything in the society or culture that you were socialized in or where you currently live that transmits irrational beliefs or thoughts or actions can be defined, in the language of public health, as an "irrational host." Common and powerful hosts and carriers of irrationality in modern society include television, popular movies, parents, teachers, politicians, religious leaders, and so on. These same hosts and carriers also transmit rationality. This is to say that television (more specifically, television writers and producers are the hosts), parents, teachers, politicians, and religious leaders are both hosts and carriers of rationality and irrationality. This means you, the target of their messages, must sort out the difference between those who are feeding you information that will help you or hurt you. Yes, you are responsible for what types of information you consume and believe and act upon.

Figure 11: Thought Virus and Remedy Thought Guide

Irrational "Thought Virus"	Rational "Remedy Thoughts"

You can begin identifying Thought Viruses by noticing what you are thinking when you are upset.

Replace your Thought Viruses with rational Remedy Thoughts. To be rational a Remedy Thought must be logical, consistent with known facts and reality, be consignee with your personal standards, help you feel the way you want to feel, help you solve your problems (or at least not make them worse,) and help you achieve your goals and realize you Vision.

All said, the solution or cure to irrationality is to decrease irrationality, increase rationality, or both. At a minimum, the ratio rationality/irrationality (R/IR) needs to be between 3:1 and 5:1, which is to say that to be "OK," you must think and behave rationally 3 to 5 times more often than you think and act irrationally. In other words, irrational thoughts and actions tend to inflict much more damage on your emotional well-being than rational thoughts and actions contribute to a healthy emotional state. These ratios are based on assumptions extrapolated from research related to how individuals, couples, and teams/groups respond to negative feedback from their environment. The assumptions are 1) over time, rationality produces positive feedback and irrationality produces negative feedback; 2) the positivity/negativity ratio (P/N), which is measured by counting the instances of positive feedback versus negative feedback from one's environment, must range from 3:1 (Losada and

Heaphy, 2004; Covello, 2009) to 5:1 (Gottman, 1994), to ensure an emotionally healthy state and positive relationships. That is, if you think and do more irrational than rational things, you are not going to be OK. This is why it should be no surprise that those who think about mostly negative things have mostly negative emotions. Conversely, those who tend to think of mostly positive things have mostly positive emotions.

Another thought replacement technique (Cognitive Reappraisal Technique) that I have developed and summarized here is called "Life Script Restructuring" (LSR).

This approach, which is described in detail in my 2014 book titled Life Script Restructuring: The Neuroplastic Psychology for Rewiring Your Brain and

Changing Your Life, is designed to help you replace irrational ways of thinking with healthier, more rational thoughts and beliefs. The primary difference that makes this approach more practical and, based on my clinical experience, more effective is the practice of replacing "stories" instead of specific thoughts.

Focusing on changing stories (Life Scripts) instead of specific thoughts is more practical because of the shear volume of thoughts that an individual thinks in a single day. It has been estimated that the average person thinks 40,000 to 70,000 thoughts each day. This makes the process of identifying and replacing specific thoughts quite tedious.

To make sense out of all these thoughts, we tend to organize them into stories. These stories are influenced by our experiences with the people we are influenced by during our developmental years, such as our parents and teachers. They help us live in and make sense of the world. They are both conscious and unconscious. And, what's most important here, these stories are both rational and irrational. The good news is that you can become aware of the conscious stories, and the irrational stories can be changed to rational ones.

Since we think thousands of thoughts each day, and organize these thoughts into stories that provide context and help us understand the world, it only makes sense that focusing on identifying, evaluating, and replacing irrational stories instead of specific irrational thoughts or beliefs (Cognitive Distortions) is more efficient and, based on my clinical experience, more effective. This is why I tend to prefer the Life Script Restructuring method over the other techniques designed to change maladaptive thinking.

Figure 12

Life Scripts Restructuring Guide

Old, Upsetting Life Scripts That I Rehearse (Irrational Stories)	New Life Scripts I Plan to Tell Myself to Overcome My Upsetting Stories

In Column 1, begin identifying and recording irrational stories (life scripts) by noticing what stories you are telling yourself when you are feeling upset. Replace these upsetting stories with life scripts that are rational. Rational stories help you feel the way you want to feel, solve your problems, achieve your goals and realize your vision.

The Life Script Restructuring technique is diagrammatically illustrated in Figure 12, which is fittingly labeled the "Life Scripts Restructuring Guide." As you can see, that you repeatedly tell yourself that, in turn, cause you to become or remain upset, in Column 1. In Column 2, you write a new rational story for each of the irrational stories you list in Column 1. More specifically, these new rational stories are what you plan to tell yourself "INSTEAD OF" the irrational stories recorded in Column 1.

As with the other techniques described above, to ensure that the new scripts are rational, you will evaluate them to ensure that they are logical and consistent with known facts and reality, help you feel the way you want to feel, contribute to a Rational Self Perception, improve a sense of well-being, solve your problems, and achieve your goals.

When I teach this approach to changing maladaptive thinking, I often use analogies from my work in Hollywood where I have observed writers changing scripts based on my input on different characters. For example, on one occasion I was meeting with a group of writers and a television producer of a popular television series where the lead character had a stage IV cancer. During our meeting, the writers and producer made the point that they had a disagreement on how the character would die. The writers wanted this character to model a more dignified dying process while the executive producer wanted her to "go out in flames" as she put it, i.e., live out her last days with reckless abandonment. They asked me what the implications would be in both scenarios. Based on my input they carried on a lively conversation, made some decisions about how the story should play out, and revised the script accordingly. After I left the studio they finalized the script and handed it off to the actress; she rehearsed until she internalized her part, and then she played the part.

All of this serves as great metaphor for Life Script Restructuring and the overall LSR process which is designed to help you create a new persona (your Rational Self Perception Vision or RSPV), write a life story or script that reflects the "new character" represented by your persona, rehearse and internalize the new script, and live a life that is rational and consistent with your goals and vision of yourself and your future. In other words, the other Cognitive Reappraisal Techniques discussed under this competency taken together with Life Script Restructuring are designed to help you, the producer of your life, write a script, rehearse it until it's believable, and then play the part. As my wife once said to me as I was explaining this analogy, "I think you are saying this means that every person is the writer and producer of their own lives, and to get different results you need to change the script—put the information together differently." My wife was right on point. The Life Script Restructuring process can help you manufacture a life that is exciting and fulfilling simply by following the steps described here.

To summarize, the techniques discussed under this competency are designed to help you systematically increase your awareness of what you are thinking and how your thinking impacts your emotions and overall rationality. All of these Cognitive Reappraisal approaches are designed to help identify and replace dysfunctional (emotionally unhealthy) thoughts with more adaptive, emotionally healthy alternatives. Furthermore, all of these techniques involve learning how to systematically 1) monitor thinking, especially during times of distress; 2) identify thoughts which are antecedents to negative emotions-the identified thoughts are called such things as Cognitive Distortions, Thought Viruses, or irrational thoughts;

3) challenge the validity of the identified maladaptive thoughts; and 4) substitute the Cognitive Distortions with more rational thoughts.

Given the fact that the undergirding principles for each of these cognitive reappraisal techniques are virtually the same, I could have used the Cognitive Distortions put forward by David Burns in his book Feeling Good, given that Cognitive Distortions, Thought Viruses, and irrational thoughts are all the same thing and are dealt with the same way in both Cognitive Restructuring and Thought Virus Replacement exercises. To illustrate how the different labels mean the same thing, I have provided a diagram (see Figure 13) that places Thought Viruses, Cognitive Distortions, Irrational Thoughts, and Irrational Life Scripts on the left side of the diagram under the label "Unhealthy Thoughts," and Remedy Thoughts, Replacement Thoughts, Rational Thoughts, and Rational Life Scripts underneath the heading entitled

"Healthy Thoughts."

Figure 13
Comparing Cognitive Reappraisal Labels Used to Describe Unhealthy and Healthy Thoughts

Labels Used to Represent Unhealthy Thoughts	Labels Used to Represent Healthy Thoughts
Thought Virus	Remedy Thought
Cognitive Distortion	Replacement Thought
Irrational Thought	Rational Thought
Irrational Life Script	Rational Life Script

Finally, before you do what is required to routinely use this competency, it's helpful to understand the logic that supports the need for consistently monitoring and mastering your internal monologue to ensure alignment between what you are thinking and your vision, goals, actions, and thoughts. This logic is shown here in Figure 14 is referred to as Mindfulness. This figure is based on the Stress Response Cycle introduced (SRC) in Section III. This version of the SRC diagrammatically illustrates that all problems (anything that causes stress) are caused by Irrational Beliefs, Irrational Thoughts, Irrational Actions, and Life Events, i.e., difficult people, places, and things that create discrepancies between expectations and reality (Cole, 2014; Cole, 1985), and the total number of problems a person experiences is directly proportionate to their level of stress. This means that anything that can be done to eliminate irrational beliefs, thoughts, and actions will, in turn, reduce the amount of distress experienced by the individual who can increase their rationality. With this in mind, as can also be seen in this diagram, the purpose of this competency is to help you eliminate your irrational beliefs, thoughts, and actions that are causing emotional distress. This doesn't mean you won't experience stress. We all have difficult stress-inducing life events (Cole, 1985) that are unavoidable. What it does mean is that through the techniques presented under this competency you can increase your "mindfulness" by decreasing the problems and distress caused by your irrational beliefs, thoughts, and actions.

Figure 14: Mindfulness in the Context of the Stress Response Cycle

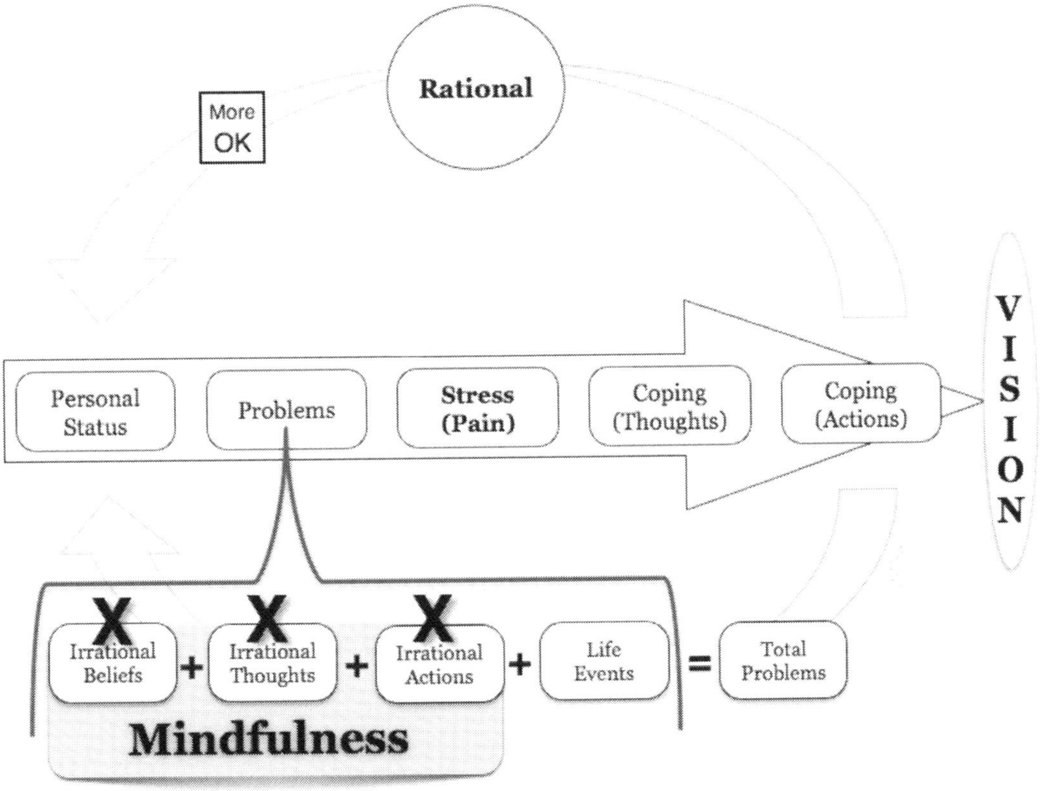

IDEAS FOR MASTERING THIS COMPETENCY

You can implement the strategies in Competency 11 by using one of the two guides that follows. I suggest that you start with the "Thought Observation and

Restructuring Guide" as a means of helping you see the connection between your emotions, beliefs, and thoughts. After learning how to use this process, I recommend that you move on to and make a habit of using the "Life Script Restructuring Guide,"

as it is easier to integrate in to your day-to-day life.

The Thought Observation and Restructuring Guide

Use the Thought Observation and Restructuring Guide to track your thoughts and emotions. Referring to the information you gathered using the "Hassle Tracker" introduced in Competency 1 should be helpful here.

Use the "Cognitive Filtering & Refinement" exercise to practice filtering out and replacing thoughts that are causing the negative emotions you record in Column 1 of the Thought Observation and Restructuring Guide to ensure that your thoughts are consistent with your vision and goals.

THOUGHT OBSERVATION AND RESTRUCTURING GUIDE: PART 1

The way you think and the things you do have an impact on your emotions and sense of well-being. If you hold on to irrational beliefs (see Reference 2) and/or you think negative thoughts, you will feel negative emotions (see Reference 1). Consequently, to decrease your negative emotions you can replace irrational beliefs and thoughts that cause unpleasant feelings with thoughts that produce more positive emotions.

The Thought Restructuring Guide is designed to help you identify and replace thoughts and thought patterns that cause unpleasant emotions. Part 1 of this guide will help you monitor and evaluate your thoughts as they relate to your negative emotions. Tables A and B below are designed to help you organize yourself as you go through this thought restructuring process.

To start the process complete the following steps: 1) monitor your emotions through-out the day; 2) record negative emotions in Column 1, Table 16a; 3) in column 2, record the time and context of what is going on at the time you notice the negative emotions; 4) determine which thoughts are associated with the emotions listed in Column 1; 5) record negative thoughts in Column 3; 6) evaluate each thought recorded in Column 3 by answering the questions in Column 4. After completing Table 16a, go on to Table 16b where you will record replacement thoughts for the irrational and distorted thoughts you have recorded in Column 3, Table 16a.

Table 16a
Negative Emotion and Thought Record

Negative Emotions (See Reference 1)	Day/Time/Event (When did I notice the negative emotion and what was going on around the same time?)	Related Thoughts (The Thoughts I Am Thinking When I Am Upset)	Evaluate My Thoughts (These Are Rules That Will Help Me Referee My Thoughts)	
			Is it Rational? (See Reference 2)	**Is it Distorted?** (See Reference 3)

REFERENCE 1

COMMON NEGATIVE EMOTIONS

> **Embarrassed, guilty, angry, sad, incompetent, afraid, anxious, hopeless, unhappy, disappointed, pessimistic, frustrated, regretful, lonely, inferior, panicky, worthless**

REFERENCE 2

IRRATIONAL THINKING

Irrational thinking includes thoughts that are not logical or based on fact, do not help you feel the way you want to feel, and do not help you overcome your problems or achieve your goals. According to behavioral scientists, the most common irrational thoughts among Americans are as follows (Albert Ellis, http://www.rebt.org. See also Competency 8.):

1. It is a dire necessity for me to be loved or approved by almost all others, who are significant to me.

2. I must be thoroughly competent, adequate, and achieving, in all important respects, in order to be worthwhile.

3. The world must be fair. People must act fairly and considerately and if they don't, they are bad, wicked, villainous, or incredibly stupid; they should be severely blamed and punished.

4. It is awful and terrible when things are not the way I very much want them to be.

5. There isn't much I can do about my anxiety, anger, depression, or unhappiness because my feelings are caused by what happens to me.

6. If something is dangerous or dreadful, I should be constantly and excessively upset about it and should dwell on the possibility of it occurring.

7. It is easier to avoid and to put off facing life's difficulties and responsibilities than face them.

8. I'm quite dependent on others and need someone stronger than myself to rely upon; I can't run my own life.

9. My past history mainly causes my present feelings and behavior; things from my past, which once strongly influenced me, will always strongly influence me.

10. I must become very anxious, angry, or depressed over someone else's problems and disturbances, if I care about that person.

11. There is a right and perfect solution to almost all problems, and it is awful not to find it.

REFERENCE 3

COGNITIVE DISTORTIONS

Irrational thoughts are sometimes labeled as Cognitive Distortions. Cognitive Distortions are patterns of thinking that produce illogical thoughts that oftentimes produce negative emotions. The 10 most common Cognitive Distortions are as follows (David Burns, Feeling Good. See Also Competency 8.):

1. **ALL OR NOTHING THINKING:** Thinking in black and white when many legitimate alternatives exist.

2. **OVER-GENERALIZATION:** Pretending that everything can be judged by a single occurrence or person. Trying to "tar everything with the same brush."

3. **MENTAL FILTER:** Seeing only the bad so you lose your perspective. Not widening your focus.

4. **DISQUALIFYING THE POSITIVE:** As it says, this is the way the mind justifies inner-philosophies that make you unhappy.

5. **JUMPING TO CONCLUSIONS (a) - MIND READING ERROR:**

6. Assuming people think a certain thing when you have no evidence for that; **(b)**

7. **FORTUNE-TELLING ERROR:** Assuming that a certain thing will happen when you've got no evidence for that.

8. **MAGNIFICATION/MINIMALIZATION:** Blowing things out of proportion or minimalizing the good aspects in yourself or a situation.

9. **EMOTIONAL REASONING:** Taking things personally when they weren't meant that way.

10. **SHOULD STATEMENTS:** Feeling things should be a certain way that you think best—and letting it get to you when they are not.

11. **LABELLING/MISLABELLING:** Labeling yourself or someone else, rather than seeing them for the whole person they are.

12. **PERSONALIZATION:** Thinking that things turn bad because you yourself are bad.

THOUGHT OBSERVATION AND RESTRUCTURING GUIDE: PART 2

The second part of this guide is designed to systematically help you replace irrational and distorted thoughts and thought patterns. Place all of the distorted and irrational thoughts you recorded in Table 16a, in Column 1 of Table 16b. Decide on new thoughts you can use to counter the irrational thoughts listed in Column 1; 2) list your replacement thoughts in Column 2; and 3) in Columns 3 and 4, respectively, develop a practice schedule for overcoming your irrational thinking. Share your progress with your therapist or with a trusted friend, pastor, or family member.

Table 16b
Thought Replacement and Practice Guide

Irrational and/or Distorted Thoughts (Taken from Column 3, in Table A)	Rational Replacement Thoughts	When and Where I Will Practice New Rational Thinking	How Often I Will Practice

The Life Script Restructuring Guide

Use the "Life Script Restructuring Guide" in Figure 12 to systematically identify stories that you tell yourself that make you upset. These stories come out of irrational beliefs that undermine your goals and your rational vision of yourself and your future. They limit your potential by dictating what you can and can't become, do, and get in life.

As with the previous exercise, the way you identify these stories is by tracking and documenting what you are telling yourself when you are upset. This means that when you are upset, you are telling yourself a story that causes you to feel bad. This also means that to change your negative emotions, you must edit or replace the stories that upset you with rational stories.

Before you begin, you should recall the section on Self-Sabotage in Section III, where it makes the point that any time you attempt to change long-held beliefs, you will experience resistance. This is because you can sometimes feel happy and fulfilled while, at the same time, still feel sad and upset because of the stories you have consistently told yourself over time; this incongruence will initially cause you to feel Change-Based Cognitive Dissonance. As you will recall from what was discussed earlier in the book (see Competency 8), this type of dissonance occurs any time you think and do things that are different than things you have thought and done in the past—like starting to exercise when you have not exercised in the past, or moving from a country where you drive on the right side of the road to a country where you drive on the left side. When this dissonance happens, simply remind yourself that this is normal and healthy and that with time and persistence it will subside.

An important thing to remember here, as with other thought restructuring techniques, is that what you say to yourself (think) determines how you feel and that your thoughts and feelings have an impact on your actions.

The point here is that if the stories you tell yourself are upsetting, you will be upset whenever you think about these stories. If you tell yourself upsetting stories over and over again, you will undoubtedly experience an array of upsetting emotions like fear, discouragement, or sadness. Fortunately, because you have control over the thoughts and personal life stories you think about, you can replace or modify thoughts and the stories you tell yourself in a way that changes the way you feel. This requires a careful analysis of what is upsetting you and reframing the thoughts that are upsetting into more rational thoughts and stories.

The process for completing the "Life Script Restructuring Guide" is somewhat self-explanatory. It involves observing your emotions throughout the day until you notice that you are upset. At that point, record the story or stories you are telling yourself in Column 1 of the guide. Once you have documented an irrational story in Column 1, write a new script or story in Column 2 that is rational in that it is logical and con-sistent with known facts and reality, helps you feel the way you want to feel, contributes to a Rational Self Perception, improves a sense of well-being, solves your problems, and achieves your goals. Rehearse the script until you believe it. Finally, any time an old, irrational story crops up, replace it with the new rational story. Do this until the old story is no longer a problem.

Another exercise you can use to master the skill of aligning your thinking with your vision, goals, and plan of action is illustrated here in the "Talk the Talk" matrix. Begin using the matrix by writing a single goal in Row 1. Then, in Column 1, record the stories you typically tell yourself that undermine this particular goal. For each story in Column 1, write a new story in Column 2 that reframes your old story into a rational story that supports your goal.

The new stories are what you will tell yourself "INSTEAD OF" the stories that undermine your goals. In Column 3, you will explain 1) "Why" you want the rational stories to come to pass, and 2) what will you plan to think and do differently to make the rational stories come true.

Finally, you will notice that the arrow on this matrix is labeled AT2R (Acknowledge

Irrational Story, and Transition 2 the Rational Story), which is designed to remind you of the action you need to take every time you start telling yourself an old story.

The logic here is that, when you are under stress that triggers an irrational story, you won't suddenly invent and start telling yourself a new, more rational story unless you have developed and practiced telling yourself this story in advance of the stressful event.

Figure 15: AT2R Change Technique

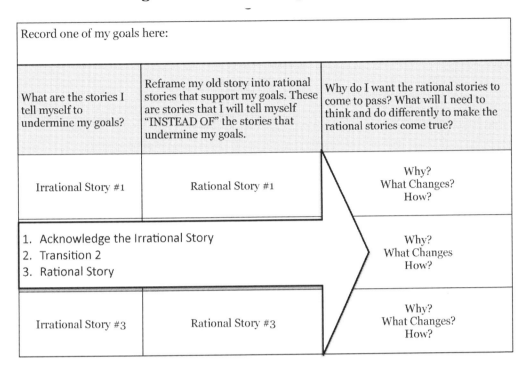

As I am sure you have already noticed, this same logic applies to all of the maladaptive thought restructuring exercises where you learn to anticipate thinking irrational thoughts and stories and prepare yourself to counter them with more adaptive thoughts. What's new here is the AT2R acronym is designed to remind you what to do when irrational thoughts and stories crop up. For example, as soon as you notice that you are thinking one of the stories you have recorded in Column 1, you will immediately say to yourself "AT2R" to remind yourself to transition to a corresponding rational story in Column 2. Obviously, this takes practice using the tools provided in Competency 10.

| My Plan for Mastering Competency 11
What will I do to master my internal monologue? |
| --- |
| |

Competency 12a & 12b

Plan to Cope Rationally and Overcome Bad Habits and Addictions

This competency has two parts: 12a and 12b. The first part, 12a, is a short review of what rational coping is and how it must be learned and applied to remain psychologically healthy. The second part, 12b, is a discussion about how to systematically document and overcome bad habits and addictions using a process that I call Counter-Flacting. These two parts are discussed under the same competency because 12b builds on the process and principles described under 12a.

12a: Rational Coping

As is illustrated in the Stress Response Cycle below, all of us experience problems that cause emotional pain, which is called stress. In fact, stress is a normal response to anything that makes us feel keyed up, threatened, or upset (Cole, 2015; Cole, Tucker & Friedman, 1990; Cole, Tucker & Friedman, 1986; Cole, 1985). This is why when we experience a problem we also experience stress.

As I explained in Section III, stress can be a good thing when it motivates us to escape from a dangerous situation or when it helps us stay energetic and alert. However, when it causes chronic psychological or physical pain, it's a message to our brain that something is wrong. This message motivates us to think or do something to get rid of the pain.

Figure 16: A Coping Plan in the Context of the Stress Response Cycle

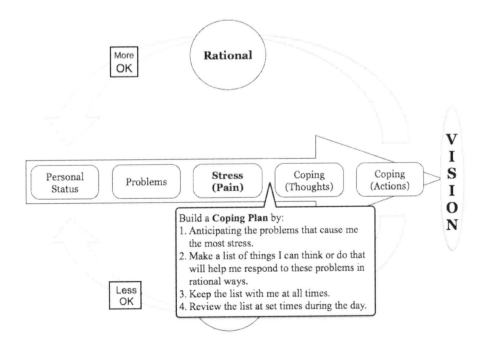

The things we think and do to get rid of this pain are called coping responses. Because stress is a form of pain and, because almost nothing focuses the mind like pain, when humans experience stress caused by a problem, they begin coping in an effort to reduce the pain. As an infant, the typical coping response to pain is to cry out. As we get older, our coping responses become more sophisticated. And, in every case, the coping responses we engage in are designed to remove the pain. For example, if we have normal sensation in our fingers and we touch a hot stove, we quickly pull back in response to the pain.

Some very important truths about coping are illustrated in the "SRC Coping Window" in Table 17. First, it should be noted that there are two broad types of coping. These can be labeled here as rational and irrational. The terms rational and irrational are interchangeable with terms like healthy and unhealthy, wise and unwise, effective and ineffective.

As can be seen in this table, both types of coping are the same with one exception. Rational coping makes an individual stronger whereas irrational coping makes a person weaker. This is one of the keys to understanding why two similar individuals who have the same problem end up in very different places. For example, the outcomes will be very different for a person who drinks alcohol to deal with stress while another person engages in aerobic exercise like running and cycling to relieve the stress-induced pain (Cole, 2015; Cole, 2014; Page & Cole, 1991; Cole, Tucker & Friedman, 1990). Admittedly, both individuals will get some relief. However, because of the addictive properties of alcohol, the person who relies on this unhealthy means of coping will need increasing higher doses of this drug to function due to tolerance and may gain weight due to the increased calories. While at the same time, the person who exercises will get the same benefit, stress reduction, as well as lose weight and gain all the benefits associated with fitness. Another example is a person who screams at his or her spouse to win an argument while another person engages in a conversation until the argument is resolved peaceably. In both cases there is relief from stress. However, in the case involving reason, the long-term outcome will be more desirable.

Table 17
SCR Coping Window

Characteristics of Rational, Healthy, Wise, Effective COPING RESPONSES	Characteristics of Irrational, Unhealthy, Unwise, Ineffective COPING RESPONSES
A way of thinking or acting in response to stress	A way of thinking or acting in response to stress
Relieves pain caused by stress	Relieves pain caused by stress

Table 17
SCR Coping Window

Characteristics of Rational, Healthy, Wise, Effective COPING RESPONSES	Characteristics of Irrational, Unhealthy, Unwise, Ineffective COPING RESPONSES
Requires mental or physical effort	Requires mental or physical effort
Requires varying degrees of discipline	Requires minimal if any discipline. Referred to as "The Path of Least Resistance," or the "Softer, Easier Path"
Oftentimes more difficult in the short term	Often easier in the short term and more difficult in the long term. Referred to as a "quick fix"
Requires internal locus of control	Rooted in external locus of control
Helps achieve rational goals	Prevents achievement of rational goals
Is moral, ethical, and legal	In some instances it's immoral, unethical, or illegal
Makes an individual stronger, healthier, wiser	Makes an individual weaker, more dependent, less wise

IDEAS FOR MASTERING THIS COMPETENCY

Table 18
Coping Planner

List the problems that have caused, or that I anticipate will cause, the most stress during my day/week/month.	What do I typically think and do in response to stress-induced by the problems listed in Column 1?	What I plan to <u>think</u> and/or <u>do</u> differently: These new coping responses should 1) help me achieve my goals, 2) have been proven to be effective, and 3) help me feel the way I want to feel.

My Plan for Mastering Competency 12(a)

How will I cope when I am under stress?
That is, what will I do INSTEAD OF those things I typically do when I am under a lot of stress?

Complete and begin implementing the "Coping Planner" in Table 18. This will help you plan new ways of coping in response to daily stressors. If you do not think about new ways of coping in response to issues you have struggled with in the past, you will not be able to change. You simply can't change the way you perform under stress unless you have thought about and practiced new ways of coping. This is all to say that "failing to plan is a way of planning to fail."

12b: Using Counter-Flacting to Overcome Bad Habits and Addictions

This section under Competency 12 introduces the competency called Counter-Flacting, which is explained in detail in my book entitled Change You: A Scientific Approach to Recovery from Bad Habits and Addictions (Cole, 2015). This process provides you with a structured approach to developing a plan to cope rationally in a way that will help you better understand and overcome bad habits and addictions. It is based on what I have experienced in my clinical practice, where, in addition to the typical addictions like alcohol, narcotics, marijuana, pornography, gambling, and the like, I have discovered that anxiety and depression can be successfully treated like bad habits and addictions. This is because they are often caused by consistently thinking and doing things that cause anxious and sad feelings. This idea makes sense to anyone who is familiar with brain plasticity and how the brain adapts itself to certain thought and behavior patterns. Just as the brain can adapt in ways that result in bad habits and addictions, because of Neuroplasticity the brain can, using the right kind of cognitive reappraisal and self-directed attention techniques, readapt to more rational, healthy thought and behavioral patterns that can permanently replace old habits.

In view of this phenomena, I developed and began to apply the approach introduced here—with great success—to a wide variety of problems, including common addictions as well as anxiety and depressive disorders. This easily understood and applied technique has been overwhelmingly successful in helping individuals overcome and recover from bad habits or addictions.

To understand the process of Counter-Flacting you will need to be familiar with the meaning of the word Flacting, which is a term created by combining the words feeling and acting. It is used to describe automatic re-actions triggered by feelings instead of rational thoughts. Accordingly, Counter-Flacting is a process designed to overcome irrational Flacting which, based on the definition I just gave you, involves overcoming or "countering" automatic reactions triggered by feelings instead of rational thoughts.

Counter-Flacting is a three-part process: 1) developing a rational vision (or a Rational Personal Vision Statement, or RPVS) of what you want in your life, as is outlined in Competency 5; 2) identifying the Irrational Flacting Routine (IFR) that makes up and defines the bad habit or addiction you want to overcome; and 3) developing and beginning to internalize a new Rational Counter-Flacting Routine (RC-FR) that you will use to replace your dysfunctional IFR. This section also relies on mental imagery, specifically referring to the Mental Movie technique, which was introduced in Competency 10. This competency will also help you adopt a practice schedule for your new RC-FR. And finally, this section provides guidance on how to conduct a "readiness check" to help you determine how prepared you are to successfully implement the C-FP. The process of replacing an IFR with a RFR requires a four-step process, which will be outlined later in this section.

The **"Mental Movie Technique"** involves watching yourself play a part by visualizing yourself practicing some activity like giving a speech, hitting a golf ball, calmly discussing a problem with your spouse, asking for a raise at work, eating a healthy diet, responding rationally to your common triggers, etc. Do this for this step in the process by:

1. Getting into a relaxed state.
2. Decide on a purpose.
3. Close your eyes and start practicing by visualizing yourself thinking and doing what you have planned to think and do in your C-FP.

Developing a Rational Personal Vision Statement

In keeping with this incredibly simple and, at the same time, incredibly important concept, the first step in the C-FP is to review your Rational Personal Vision Statement or (RPVS), which you created in Competency 5. For purposes of convenience, I will once again walk you through the steps required to create a RPVS in the context of this Counter-Flacting exercise.

As I mentioned under Competency 5, your RPVS represents a rational (based on objective truth), optimistic, broad-based, mental model of your highest and best self and of a bright and promising future. In keeping with the idea of "starting with the end in mind," the vision you articulate here represents the end goal of the coping thoughts and actions you decide to adopt and apply as an integral part of your C-FP.

Figure 17: RPVS at the Point of the SRC Decision Point

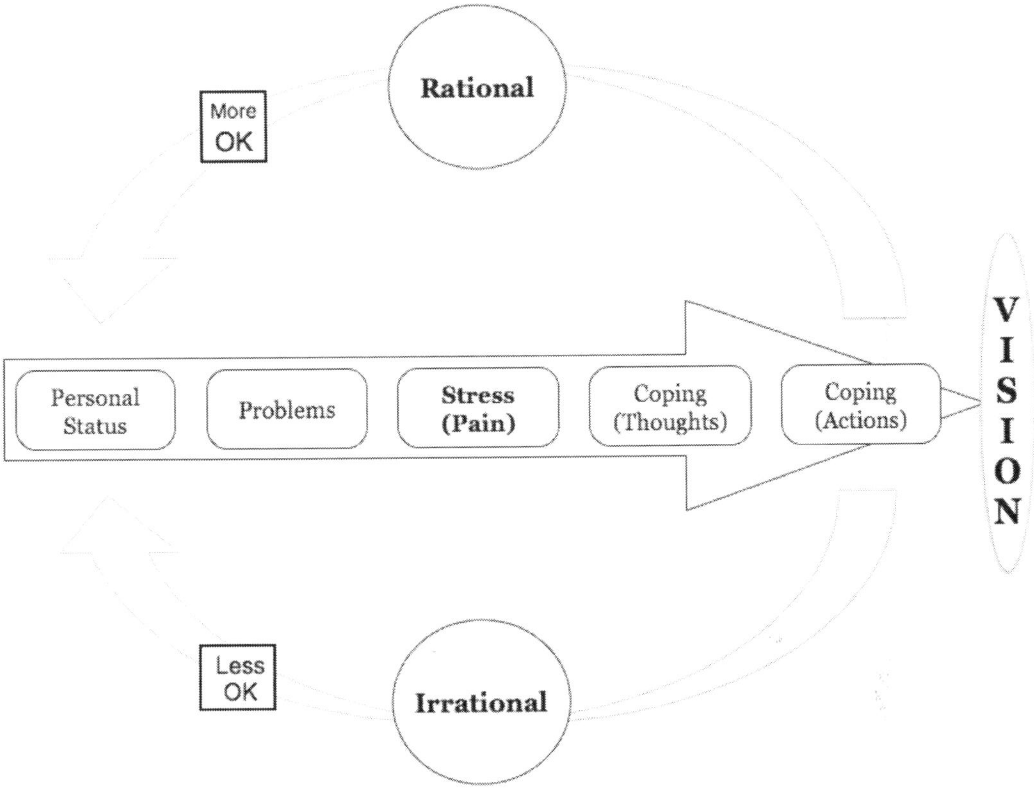

To diagrammatically illustrate how the RPVS fits into the CF-P, I have provided an updated diagram of the Stress Response Cycle (SRC) with an image of a RPVS, labeled as Vision, placed on the far right side of the diagram (Figure 16). The RPVS is strategically placed near the "Decision Point" on the SRC because a clear vision of what you want in life has an influence on your coping decisions and represents what it is that you are striving toward as you develop a strategy that includes more rational ways of thinking and acting. The point here is that if you have no explicit vision or if the vision of what you want in life is unclear, it will have little or no influence on your decision-making process. On the other hand, a clear vision of what you want in life can have a profound influence on all of your decisions, including what you decide to think and do in response to problem-induced stress and pain that is triggering and sustaining the bad habit or addiction that you are trying to overcome with the CF-P.

There are many benefits to developing an RPVS. For example, because your RPVS will articulate what your "ideal" self and life will look like after you have overcome a bad habit or an addiction, your RPVS can serve as a yardstick to measure your current situation and your progression toward or digression away from what you are trying to

> *If you don't know where you are going then it doesn't matter which road you take.*
>
> ## Alice in Wonderland

Unlike a goal, once you have created it, your RPVS will rarely change. This is because it represents the very essence of who you are, who you want to become, and your reasons (your "WHYs") for the way you want to experience and see yourself and your future. In short, you are manufacturing a new perspective. When you adopt this new perspective, you will start to notice that your thoughts and actions will begin to align with this new outlook which, in turn, will help you begin to leave behind your old irrational ways of thinking and acting.

As I explained in Competency 5, your RPVS should have a positive tone. This is because the way you see yourself and your future impacts everything you think and do. Above all, it impacts your level of happiness and sense of serenity.

If your vision of self and your future is depicted in negative ways, your thoughts, behaviors, and state of happiness will be impacted negatively. Conversely, if you choose to think or do things that cause you to see yourself and your future in more positive ways, your life will be influenced in a positive direction. Lasting happiness only comes to those who think and do what it takes to attain an image of themselves and their future that is rational.

In Competency 5, you created a Rational Personal Vision Statement to help you become the person you want to be—someone who is rational, can overcome challenges, and can reach goals that lead to lifelong happiness. The purpose of Competency 12 is to engage your RPVS to help you overcome and change limiting stories you tell yourself about yourself (also defined as Life Scripts in Competency 11) that may be negative or irrational. A positive RPVS naturally contains positive Life Scripts and focuses on your abilities and your future potential so that you can become the kind of person who does the kinds of things you want to do in life.

As you begin this process, it's useful to remember that the objective here is to design a prototype RPVS that represents the best possible person you can become (given the real, instead of the perceived, limits on your potential) while living the best possible life you can live. In other words, the RPVS you develop and evaluate should represent what you want to become, do, feel, think, own, associate with, and impact by some date in the future.

I have included the steps for designing and testing a RPVS that I first introduced in Competency 5. These steps include the following:

1. Review the following "Visioning Questions" to help you begin thinking about what you want to put into your RPVS:

- What inspires me? What do I want my life to stand for?

- If I could fix one problem in the world what would it be? What would I do about this problem?

- What are my most important values?

- What are the main things that motivate me/bring me joy and satisfaction?

- What are my two best moments I have experienced in the past ten years?

- What three things would I do if I won a 200 million dollar lottery?

- What are my greatest strengths/abilities/traits/things I do best?

- What are at least two things I can start doing/do more often that use my strengths and bring me joy?

- What are at least two things I can start thinking that will bring me greater happiness?

- What are at least two things I would like to stop doing or do as little as possible?

- If a miracle occurred and my life was just as I wanted it to be, what would be different?

2. Use the "Rational Personal Vision Statement Guide" in Table 19 to: a) identify pictures or images that represent the things you want to BEcome, Do, or Get—taken together, these images will represent your ideal RPVS; b) briefly explain how each image represents something you want; c) describe the reason "WHY" you want these things; and d) after you have described what you want and WHY, decide on one "Cue Word" that represents each of the images making up your RPVS.

3. Use the "RPVS Rationality Guide" to evaluate and identify elements in your RPVS that are irrational.

4. Revise the irrational elements in your RPVS.

5. Repeat steps 2 and 3 until all elements in your RPVS are rational.

We are what we repeatedly do. Excellence, then, is not an act, but a habit. Aristotle

Table 19
Rational Personal Vision Guide

Identify 10 pictures or images that represent what you want to BE, DO, GET. After you have finished this step, these images will represent your Rational Personal Vision Statement. Briefly 1) explain how each image represents something you want to BE (calm, successful, thin, on time, confident, faithful, disciplined, fun, trustworthy, etc.), DO (graduate from college, get married, travel around the world, write a book, etc.) and GET (a new car or home, great job, a boat, etc.). Then describe the reason WHY you want the things represented by each picture. After you have described how you want to see yourself and your future, and WHY, decide on 1 "Cue Word" that represents each of the images making up your RPVS.

IMAGE 1	I want to... The reasons WHY are...	Cue Word 1
IMAGE 2	I want to... The reasons WHY are...	Cue Word 2
IMAGE 3	I want to... The reasons WHY are...	Cue Word 3
IMAGE 4	I want to... The reasons WHY are...	Cue Word 4
IMAGE 5	I want to... The reasons WHY are...	Cue Word 5
IMAGE 6	I want to... The reasons WHY are...	Cue Word 6
IMAGE 7	I want to... The reasons WHY are...	Cue Word 7
IMAGE 8	I want to... The reasons WHY are...	Cue Word 8
IMAGE 9	I want to... The reasons WHY are...	Cue Word 9
IMAGE 10	I want to... The reasons WHY are...	Cue Word 10

Figure 18: RVSP Rationality Guide

Ask each element (represented by an image and cue word) in your initial Rational Personal Vision Statement (RPVS) the following questions. If you answer no to any of these questions it's likely that the element you are considering is irrational. Revise the irrational elements until you can answer yes to every question. Feel free to add to or take away from the questions provided here.

If I fully adopt this element in my Rational Personal Vision Statement, will I:

- reach my full potential?

- become the kind of person I want to be?

- achieve my short- and long-term goals?

- learn from my past, prepare for my future, and live in the present?

- have the ability to think and act in terms of principles and not emotions?

- perceive myself as someone who is in control of my destiny?

- be able to solve my problems and ask others for help when I need it?

- feel secure about who I am, and not feel insecure when others question how I see myself and live my life?

- be able to evaluate what others think and feel against my own standards, and have the courage to act according to my own convictions, regardless of what others do or say?

- feel secure enough about my beliefs that I can change them in the face of new facts?

- be able to exercise self-control by stoping, thinking, and making rational decisions?

- look beyond the surface, find real meaning, and weigh the pros and cons of an event or issue?

- wait for things that I want even when this requires patience and delaying immediate gratification?

- keep trying, even when things don't go the way I would like them to?see myself as someone who is equal in value to others, rather than inferior or superior, while accepting differences in my abilities, socio-economic standing, and personal potential?

- respect and obey the laws that are rational in that they are fair and just?

- respect the dignity of all men and women, without respect to religion, race, or gender?

Identifying the Irrational Flacting Routine

As I mentioned earlier, Flacting is a word made up by combining the words feeling and acting. This term is used to describe automatic re-actions triggered by feelings instead of conscious thoughts.

Flacting can be either rational or irrational, depending on the automatic actions that follow the feeling. In other words, if you automatically respond to a trigger in a way that helps you achieve your goals and realize your personal vision, the Flacting is considered rational. Conversely, if your automatic reactions undermine your ability to reach your goals and realize your personal vision, these reactions are irrational.

Figure 18: Irrational Coping Routine in the Context of the SRC

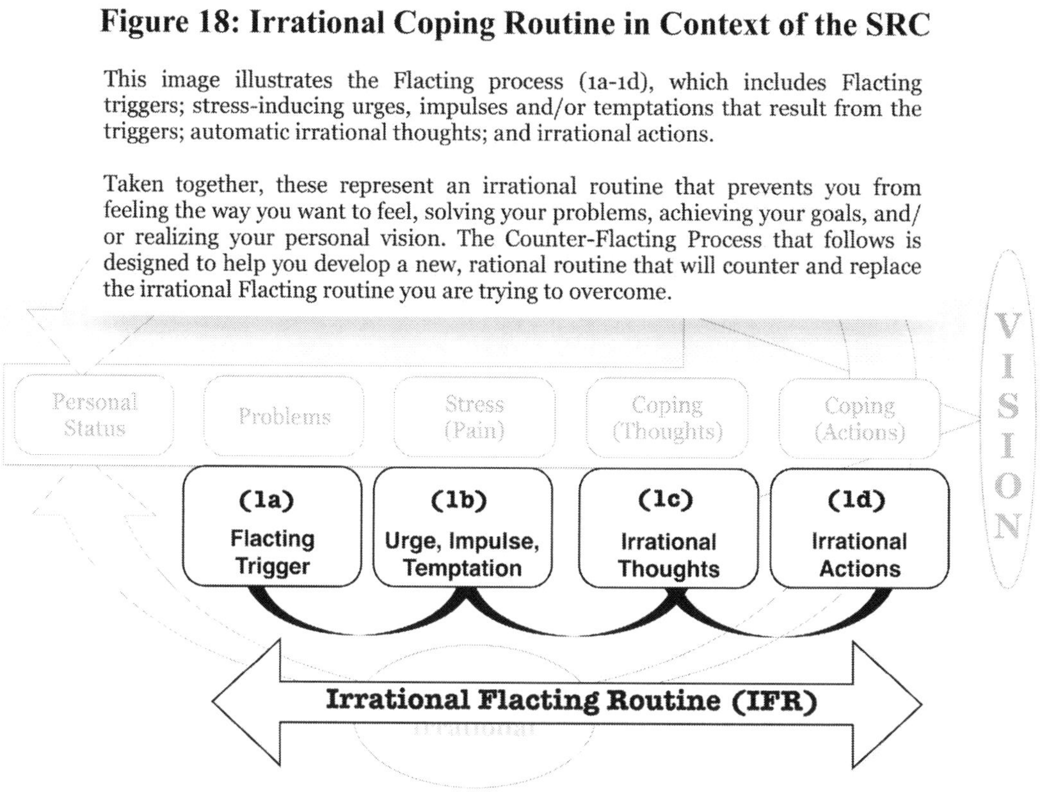

Figure 18: Irrational Coping Routine in Context of the SRC

This image illustrates the Flacting process (1a-1d), which includes Flacting triggers; stress-inducing urges, impulses and/or temptations that result from the triggers; automatic irrational thoughts; and irrational actions.

Taken together, these represent an irrational routine that prevents you from feeling the way you want to feel, solving your problems, achieving your goals, and/or realizing your personal vision. The Counter-Flacting Process that follows is designed to help you develop a new, rational routine that will counter and replace the irrational Flacting routine you are trying to overcome.

This step in the C-FP is designed to help you identify the Irrational Flacting Routine (IFP), or the bad habit or addiction that you want to overcome. Figure 18 shows variables that make up this routine superimposed over the Stress Response Cycle (SRC). This image illustrates the Flacting process (1a-1d), which includes 1a) Flacting triggers; 1b) stress-inducing urges, impulses, and/or temptations that result from exposure to the triggers; 1c) automatic irrational thoughts; and 1d) irrational actions. Taken together, these four steps represent an irrational routine that, by definition, prevents you from feeling the way you want to feel, solving your problems, achieving your goals, and/or realizing what you have outlined in your RPVS. In short, this is the anatomy of the bad habit or addiction that you want to overcome.

The following steps will help you explain this Irrational Flacting Process in a way that prepares you to develop a Counter-Flacting Process (C-FP) that strikes at the root cause of the problem you are trying to overcome and replaces irrational thoughts and actions with rational ones.

STEP 1a: The Flacting Trigger

While considering the problem you are trying to overcome (the specific bad habit or addiction), list the people, places, and things (the triggers) that cause you to start thinking, feeling, and doing things that are related to or directly causing the bad habit or addiction you are trying to overcome.

_____

_____

_____

STEP 1b: Urges, Impulses, and Temptations

In this step you will begin to identify the automatic emotional responses you experience when you are triggered by those people, places, and things listed in Step 1a. This information will help you begin to understand what is driving your problem by providing you with another link (the emotional component) in the causal chain of events running from the root cause of the problem you are experiencing and its symptoms. This information is vital in the step of the C-FP where you develop an Emotional Regulation Plan that will help you begin to literally break the chain that is binding you to your problem. (The Emotional Regulation Plan will be discussed in more detail in Step 3b.)

To begin the process of understanding and intervening in your emotional reactions that encourage irrational Flacting, list in the space provided below all of the upsetting urges, impulses, and temptations you experience in response to the triggers you listed in Step 1a:

_____

_____

_____

STEP 1c: Irrational Thoughts and Stories

In this step you will identify irrational thoughts you think or stories that you tell yourself (also referred to as Life Scripts in my previous work; Cole, 2014) in response to negative triggers, upsetting urges, impulses, and temptations you have recorded in Steps 1a-1b. Irrational thoughts and stories are things you think and/or tell yourself that are not logical and/or there is no evidence to support them as being true, do not help you feel the way you want to feel, do not help you overcome your problems, and/or undermine your goals and prevent you from realizing your RPVS. List these irrational thoughts and stories below:

_____

_____

_____

STEP 1d: Irrational Actions

In this step you will record all of your irrational actions in response to your irrational thoughts recorded in Step 1c. Irrational actions (or behaviors) are observable things you do that make up the bad habit or addiction you are trying to overcome. By definition, irrational actions are not logical, do not help you feel the way you want to feel, do not help you overcome your problems, and/or undermine your goals and your ability to realize your RPVS.

At this point, list all of your irrational actions that are related to the problem you are trying to overcome. Ask others who know you for ideas; since these behaviors are often automatic, you may not be consciously aware of them:

_____

_____

_____

Developing and Beginning to Internalize a New Rational Counter-Flacting Routine

The next step in developing a personal self-directed change plan that uses the C-FP is to develop a Rational Counter-Flacting Routine or RC-FR. The RC-FR is the process that retrains your thoughts and actions so that you can adopt and internalize a new Rational Flacting Routine. This routine will be carefully tailored to replace your bad habits and addictions, which are referred to as Irrational Flacting Routine (IFR). Once you develop your new routine, you will use the activities I have described in this section to internalize your new Rational Flacting Routine. In other words, this new routine will become what you think and do, going forward, INSTEAD OF your old routine, which constituted the bad habit or addiction you are striving to overcome. Your routine will become automatic because an essential part of this step is to practice or rehearse the new routine until it's second nature.

From a point of logic, all of this is necessary for at least two reasons. First, if you do not have a carefully thought-out routine that you can engage in INSTEAD OF your old routine, when you are triggered you will not have any place to go except back to your old, "tried and true" routine that you have used to cope with problem-induced stress over and over again until it has become a bad habit or addiction. And secondly, if you do not practice the new routine until it becomes automatic, you will revert back to your old ways of doing things because, as I just said, you have practiced them until they have become automatic responses (Irrational Flacting Routines) that do not require any thought when you are triggered. That said, Steps 2a-4c, which are illustrated here in Figure 19 will carefully guide you through the process of developing a Rational Counter-Flacting Plan that includes a relevant goal, a new Rational Flacting Routine that will replace your old Irrational Flacting Routine, and a schedule for practicing your new routine until it becomes automatic.

Figure 19: Rational Counter-Flacting Routine

Figure 19: Rational Counter-Flacting Routine

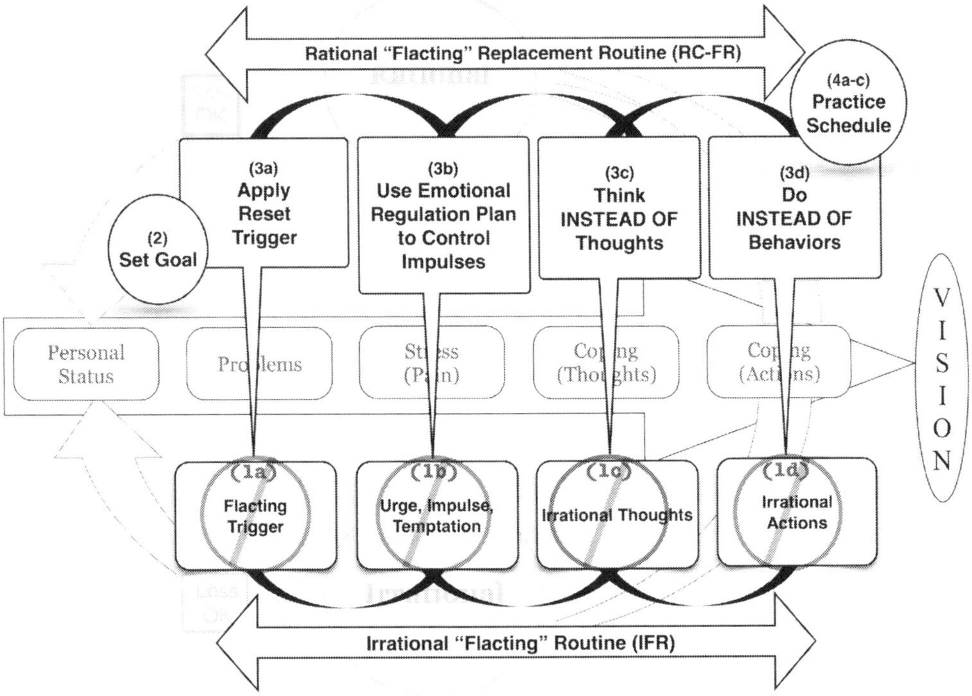

STEP 2: Set a Counter-Flacting Goal

Set a goal that you can reach using the C-FP (your new routine). Your goal should describe what you want to achieve. The conscious process of identifying and writing down a goal is what will help you succeed in creating, learning, and consistently applying the new Counter-Flacting Routine. As you have already learned, your goal should be specific, measurable, realistic, and stated in terms of a distinct time period. (You may want to refer to Competency 6 to review how to set and reach attainable goals.) Answering the following questions will help you do this.

What will be different about me and my life if I successfully change?

_____

_____

When will I complete my goal (some date in the future)? ___/___/___

How will I demonstrate and evaluate the extent to which my goal has been met? In other words, how will I know I am different?

_____

_____

What will I do to achieve my goal?

_____I will consistently implement my Counter-Flacting Plan_____

_____

_____

STEP 3a: Decide on a Reset Trigger

Decide on a "Reset Trigger" by doing the following: 1) spend some time thinking about the upsetting thoughts or stories you tell yourself to justify continuing the bad habit or addiction you are trying to overcome; 2) summarize all of these upsetting stories in a single sentence, like a newspaper headline; 3) represent the headline with an abstract mental image like cloudy or murky or dreary or sharp or jagged or dark or rusty or glaring, etc.; 4) think about your vision (meaning, what you really want and what things would be like if you were your highest and best self); and then 5) decide on a symbol (like a wild bird or another animal—your mind will pick the perfect symbol) that represents your vision of what you want and what your life will be like when you are at your best and have overcome your bad habit or addiction. Write the abstract mental image in Column 1 of Table 20 and then record your chosen symbol in Column 2. From this point on, when you are triggered by whatever is represented by the abstract image you have written in Column 1, think instead about your symbol in Column 2, which is now your Reset Trigger. If you like, you can go through this process more than once to identify different Reset Triggers for different problems. This type of specificity can be very helpful.

Table 20
Reset Trigger Identification Guide

My Headline & Abstract Image	My Vision & Reset Trigger (My Symbol)

STEP 3b: Develop an Emotional Regulation Plan

Develop an "Emotional Regulation Plan" to manage and control your emotions while you prepare to implement your new Rational Counter-Flacting Routine (RC-FR). For example, your plan for controlling your emotions when you experience an impulse, urge, or temptation to Flact could be to breathe for 20 seconds, and then say to yourself a) I'm upset, b) this is an opportunity for me to get stronger (because every time I practice this new routine when triggered, I become better at it), and c) I will get stronger by applying my INSTEAD OFs.

There are many different things you can do to regulate your emotions until you are ready to start thinking and doing what is outlined in your new RC-FP. These techniques are laid out in Table 21.

Table 21
Emotional Regulation Technique Options

Self-Talk: a) Breathe in through your nose and out through your mouth (exaggerating the exhale) for 20 seconds, b) say to yourself "I'm upset or tempted," c) "This is an opportunity to become stronger by practicing my new routine," and d) apply your new INSTEAD OF thoughts and actions.

Distract Yourself: Pick up a magazine and focus your attention on the pictures or an interesting article. Focus your mind on whatever you are reading or looking at, redirecting it from upsetting thoughts and feelings.

Self-Soothe: Slowly drink your favorite beverage (soda, juice, hot chocolate, water), focusing on the sensations of taste, smell, and temperature. Or take a hot shower or bath.

Intense Sensations: Go to the kitchen and take a piece of ice and some napkins. Hold the ice in your hand, and use the napkins to absorb the melting water. Focus on the intense cold sensation of ice in your hand.

Practice Deep Breathing: Get in a relaxed position and breathe in and out while telling yourself something like, "I breathe in relaxation and breathe out stress."

Use Relaxation: Give yourself a little neck and shoulder massage. You can rapidly tap your fingers on your neck and shoulders or rub your neck and shoulders. Focus on different muscles in your body from your head to your feet, telling yourself to let go of tightness and tension.

Pray: Say the Serenity Prayer, or pray according to your religious practice.

Self-Encouragement: Think of what you might say to someone in a similar situation as you. Give yourself the same encouragement and support. Tell yourself things like "You can get through this" or "This won't last forever."

Use Imagery: Imagine a peaceful, secure place, while thinking about all the things that make you happy or calm or effective.

Focus on Thought or Redundant Routines:

Smartphone App Distraction:

Irrational Thought Replacement Guide

Focus on Thought or Redundant Routines: Count backwards from 50. If you lose track, start over again. Make a to-do list. Describe the furniture in the room or other objects in front of you.

Smartphone App Distraction: Angry birds, plants and zombies, dots, bubbles; Facebook, Pinterest, Google+, Instagram, LinkedIn, etc.

Listen to a favorite song on the radio, to passing traffic, or to a relaxation or hypnosis Application on your phone.

Watch a TV program, a video on your smartphone, or a funny short on YouTube or Facebook.

STEP 3c: Decide on New, Rational "INSTEAD OF" Thoughts

This step involves deciding on thoughts you can think or stories you can tell yourself that counter your irrational thoughts and stories that you recorded in Column 1.

These new thoughts and stories are considered rational if they are logical and based on truth and if they help you feel the way you want to feel (over the long run), solve your problems, achieve your goals, and realize your RPVS.

Begin this step by transferring the irrational thoughts you recorded in Step 1c to Column 1 in Table 22. Next, record your new rational thoughts and stories in Column 2. These new thoughts are things you will think INSTEAD OF the thoughts you used to think (those listed in Column 1).

Table 22
Irrational Thought Replacement Guide

Old, Irrational Thoughts (Stories, Life Scripts)	New, "INSTEAD OF" Replacement Thoughts, Stories, Scripts

STEP 3d: Decide on New, Rational "INSTEAD OF" Behaviors

This step helps you identify rational actions that you will plan to engage in, INSTEAD OF the behaviors you identified in Step 1d. Transfer the irrational actions you recorded in Step 1d to Column 1 in Table 23. Finally, decide on a number of new actions you can engage in INSTEAD OF those things you have done in the past (those listed in Column 1). Record these new actions in Column 2.

Table 23
Irrational Behavior Replacement Guide

Old, Irrational Behaviors	New, "INSTEAD OF" Replacement Behaviors

On one occasion when I was meeting in a clinical setting with a particularly resistant client, he asked me, "What is there to do after work besides drink?" I said, "There are many things to do." He said, "Give me one good example." At that point I walked to the chalkboard in my office and I quickly listed many things (I had done this several times before so it was easy) under the title, "Some examples of new actions you can do INSTEAD OF the irrational actions." Some of these things included finishing a project or starting a new one; planning how to build or strengthen your career; collecting things; soaking in a bathtub; calling a friend; singing a favorite song; making someone a gift; writing a note to a friend; going swimming; playing cards or a board game; skating; flying a kite; going on a date; going to a lake; repairing something; working on a car; writing in your diary; practicing yoga, karate, or archery; lifting weights; going fishing; walking up and down the stairs 10 times; thinking about your best vacation/best trip; thinking of a favorite thing to do; reading your favorite quotes; breathing through your nose and out through your mouth 10 times; taking an ice cold shower or a hot bath; listening to calming or distracting music; reading scriptures or other inspirational text; petting a dog or a cat; holding ice in your hand; or playing a game on your smartphone.

Once I finished the list, my client said, "I really don't like to do any of those things!" I responded, "Not even taking a bath?" And he said, "That's right, not even taking a bath!" I said, "OK, what do you like to do?" Can you guess what he said? Yep, he said, "I like to drink." Unfortunately, this fellow liked to drink so much that he lost his job and his wife and ended up living with his elderly mother and spending lots of time drinking. Hopefully, you will try harder than this person to come up with things you can think and do INSTEAD OF those things that have become bad habits or addictions.

STEP 4a: Develop a Practice Schedule

This step calls for developing a schedule for practicing your new RC-FR, which is made up of Steps 3a-3d. The plan needs to specify how and when you will practice and for how long. Because of what we know about brain plasticity, I recommend that you practice at least two times per day, for 66 consecutive days.

I recommend that you use the Mental Movie Technique (Maltz, 1960) to practice your new routine. This technique (first introduced in Competency 10) involves closing your eyes and imagining yourself watching a movie that includes your RPVS and your newly created RC-FR. As you watch these ideas in your "mind's eye," use your imagination to see yourself thinking and doing what is required to a) accomplish what is outlined in your vision, and b) respond to your Flacting Triggers with your new Counter-Flacting Routine. Do this over and over again until the new rational routine becomes automatic.

The **"Mental Movie Technique"** involves watching yourself play a part by visualizing yourself practicing some activity like giving a speech, hitting a golf ball, calmly discussing a problem with your spouse, asking for a raise at work, eating a healthy diet, responding rationally to your common triggers, etc. Do this for this step in the process by:
1. Getting into a relaxed state.
2. Decide on a purpose.
3. Close your eyes and start practicing by visualizing yourself thinking and doing what you have planned to think and do in your C-FP.

Anticipating and Overcoming Barriers to Change

Another important consideration here has to do with the barriers you will undoubtedly encounter in the process of developing, practicing, and ultimately adopting your new routine. I suggest that you use Table 24 to systematically to consciously anticipate and make plans to overcome these barriers. You can do this by listing the barriers (people, places, or things) and rationalizations that may prevent you from developing or implementing your C-FP in Column 1. In Column 2 of Table 24, list what you will think and/or do to overcome your barriers and counter your rationalizations to successfully achieve your Counter-Flacting goal (which you set in Step 2 of this competency).

Table 24
Guide for Overcoming Barriers to Change

Anticipate and list the barriers (people, places, or things) and rationalizations that may prevent me from developing or implementing my Counter-Flacting plan.	What I will think and/or do to overcome my barriers and counter my rationalizations to successfully achieve my Counter-Flacting goals.

STEP 4b: Check Your Readiness

In this step you present your new Rational Counter-Flacting Routine to someone you know and trust to give you honest, supportive feedback. This could be your therapist, spouse, friend, sponsor, or religious leader. Once you have identified the appropriate person and he or she has agreed to help, ask this person to use the "Counter-Flacting Accountability Scale," in Table 25, to help you determine how prepared you are to use your C-FP to overcome your habit or addiction. This person will help you determine if you have met the standards for each of the Standards of Success by doing what is called for in Column 2 of the Counter-Flacting Accountability Scale. Your support person can do this by turning each one of the standards in Column 2 into a question. For example, the first standard could be converted into the following question, "Have you developed a goal that is Specific-target a specific area for improvement; Measurable-quantify or at least suggest an indicator of progress; Realistic-state what results can realistically be achieved, given available resources, and Time-related-specify when the result(s) can be achieved?"

You will note in Column 3 there is a corresponding score for each of the standards. If, for example, you answer yes to the question I just posed about Standard 1, you would get 1 point. Accordingly, have your support person review each standard and provide you a total score. A score of 10 means you are totally prepared. If do not score 10, go back and do whatever is required to become totally prepared. Do not start until you have completed a comprehensive plan using the C-FP in its entirety.

Step 4c: Practice Your Counter-Flacting Routine

This is where you begin practicing your new routine. To ensure that this happens, it helps to carry your new Counter-Flacting Routine with you at all times. Use the Mental Movie Technique to practice the new Counter-Flacting Routine as is outlined in Step 4a (your Practice Schedule).

Table 26
Counter-Flacting Plan Summary

Counter-Flacting STEPS	Summarize Your Plan Here
Goal (Step 2)	
Reset Trigger (3a)	
Emotional Regulation Plan (Step 3b)	
INSTEAD OF Thoughts (Step 3c)	
INSTEAD OF Behaviors (Step 3d)	
Practice Schedule (Step 4a)	
Barriers	
How you plan to overcome barriers.	

Based on my clinical experience, the best way to master Competency 12b (Using Counter-Flacting to Overcome Bad Habits and Addictions) is to summarize everything you plan to do in a single document that you can refer to as you implement your plan. To help you with this I have provided the "Counter-Flacting Plan Summary" in Table 26. This form will help you summarize the information you will need to consistently practice and apply your plan in a way that will leverage brain plasticity and help you make changes.

Competency 13
Evaluate Your Progress and Adjust Your Plan of Action

This final competency helps you set up a process for monitoring your performance and progress. This process will help you identify and better understand the "hows" and "whys" behind your failures and successes. This understanding will enable you to overcome your failures and replicate your success over and over again.

Evaluating yourself is to your success because a perfectly designed and executed approach is a waste of time and energy if it is not implemented as planned (Cole, 1999). To do this requires some understanding of how to set and measure your progress against performance standards (Cole, Pogostin, Westover, Rios & Collier, 1995).

Performance standards are those expectations you have concerning how you want to go about achieving your goals and realizing your vision. When you evaluate your performance, you compare what you want or expect your performance to be (the performance standard) against what you actually think or do. If there is considerable discrepancy between what you want to think and do as compared to what you actually think and do, then you are under performing.

Poor performance typically results when you are not fully committed to your goal, you are not clear about what the goal is, you don't clearly articulate the steps you need to take to achieve your goal, or you don't have something (e.g., knowledge, skills, motivation, equipment, or support) that is required to carry out the steps in your plan, etc. With this in mind, you will used the methods described in this competency to 1) evaluate how you are doing by comparing what you have laid out in your goals and plan of action against what you are actually doing; and 2) if there is a discrepancy, hold yourself accountable. That is, admit you are not performing as planned and make whatever changes are necessary to your plan or your performance to get back on track.

IDEAS FOR MASTERING THIS COMPETENCY

The following ideas will help you develop a plan to determine how you are doing and what you need to change to improve your performance. Essentially, this involves asking yourself questions that provide you insight into whether or not you are doing what you plan to think and do to achieve your goals. Some specific questions that you may want to routinely ask yourself include:

- Am I making progress toward my goal?

- What am I doing that is going well and why?

- What am I doing that isn't working and why?

- What could I do better with a little tweaking?

- What should I stop doing so I can do other things?

- Where is my time most being wasted?

- What discipline do I most need to implement into my day?

- What drains my energy just to think about doing again?

- What changes do I need to make?

Another set of questions that can help you gain further insight into what you need to change to improve your performance consider what you might think or do more or less of to improve. These questions include:

- What do I need to think more about to achieve this goal?

- What do I need to think less about to achieve this goal?

- What do I need to do more of to achieve this goal?

- What do I need to do less of to achieve this goal?

- Where do I need to spend more time?

- Where do I need to spend less time?

- Whom should I spend more time with?

- Whom should I spend less time with?

- What will prevent me from thinking and doing these things (knowledge, skills, motivation)?

- Who may prevent me from doing these things?

Finally, use the "Evaluation Planning Guide" in Table 27 as a model for developing a system you can use to track and document your progress (Cole, 1999). In Column 1, list the goals you plan to track with this guide. In Column 2, record the action steps you plan to carry out to achieve each goal. In Column 3, describe how you will know whether or not you can carry out each action step and achieve your goals. Lastly, in Column 4, document your successes and failures. When you document failures, record what you plan to think or do differently to get back on track toward your goals.

Table 27
Evaluation Planning Guide

What Goals do I Plan to Track?	What Action Steps Do I Plan to Track?	How Will I Know if I Carry Out My Action Steps and Achieve My Goals? (My Performance Standards)	Document My Successes and Failures: What Will I Think or Do Differently to Overcome Failures?

My Plan for Mastering Competency 13

How will I track my progress and make necessary adjustments to ensure my success?

SECTION V
Self-Directed Change Planner

Finally, in the spirit of the quote by Einstein where he said, "Make everything as simple as possible, but not simpler," Section V of the book provides you with another shortcut to self-improvement. Based on my experience in helping people change, I have learned that without detailed, specific information for action, the good intentions of most individuals will remain just that—good intentions. With this in mind, this final section provides you with very detailed information laid out in a process that is easy to understand and apply.

The Self-Directed Change Planner (S-DCP) introduced here guides you through a number of steps that incorporate and integrate the principles and competencies laid out in the previous sections. Similar to the Counter-Flacting approach outlined in Competency 12b, as you respond to each step you will be developing a plan that you will use, on a day-to-day basis, to help you remember exactly what you plan to change and how you plan to maintain the change, including how you will identify triggers, overcome barriers, and achieve your most important goals. As I advised during the competencies, if you need more space to record your responses, please use your journal.

A) DETERMINE WHAT YOU WANT TO CHANGE.

Self-Improvement requires changing your behavior by either 1) adding a positive behavior like exercise or 2) eliminating a negative behavior like oversleeping. To begin self-improvement, select the behavior you want to change. Evaluate the behavior to ensure the change you plan to make is consistent with your personal standards of right and wrong (and your RPVS). If the change requires you to go against your personal standards, then select another behavior to work on. If the behavior does fit, go on to the next step.

B) MAKE A COMMITMENT TO YOURSELF BY WRITING A CHANGE GOAL.

I will (describe the behavior you plan to add or eliminate)

_____

_____

_____

on or before (date by which you will have maintained this change for at least 66 days)_____. I will begin preparing for this change on _____. I will have completed my preparation by _____. I will begin changing on (date)_____.

C) PREPARE TO CHANGE.

List the things you need to begin and maintain the change. These items include obtaining information (from a credible source), skills, resources (equipment, food, books), permission, etc. Also, list where or from whom you will get these things, and when you will get them. If possible, interview someone, read a book about someone, or watch a movie about someone who made a similar change.

WHAT DO I NEED?

WHERE OR FROM WHOM WILL I GET WHAT I NEED?

WHEN WILL I GET THESE THINGS?

D) DEVELOP YOUR <u>FIRST</u> PLAN FOR CHANGE.

List the steps (small, realistic, achievable) for improvement. Also indicate when you will take these steps (e.g., several times a day, daily, or weekly).

WHAT I WILL DO?

WHEN I WILL DO IT?

E) GET SUPPORT FOR CHANGE.

Although the change process is ultimately your responsibility, it can be very helpful to get support from others. Ask one or more people to help you improve. Those who agree to participate should read and sign your improvement strategy.

1) I (name of supporter)_____, agree to provide support and encouragement to (your name)_____, in his or her efforts to make the change described above. My support will include:_____.

2) I (name of supporter) _____, agree to provide support and encouragement to (your name) _____, in his or her efforts to make the change described above. My support will include:_____.

F) PLAN TO REWARD YOURSELF WHEN YOU MAKE CHANGES.

Rewarding your changes can help you maintain the change. Develop a list of rewards (that are inexpensive and unrelated to food or drugs/alcohol) that you can treat yourself to upon completing each step in your improvement process. Indicate when you will get rewards and under what conditions.

G) VISUALIZE AND LIST THE BENEFITS OF MAKING THIS CHANGE.

Visualizing the benefits (positive outcomes) you expect to gain from making this change will motivate you and help you to remain focused on what you want to accomplish. List these benefits here:

_____
_____
_____

H) VISUALIZE AND LIST THE NEGATIVE CONSEQUENCES OF NOT MAKING THIS CHANGE.

Visualizing the negative outcomes you could face if you do not make this change will motivate you and help you to remain focused on what you do want to accomplish. List these possible negative outcomes here:

_____

_____

_____

I) ANTICIPATE AND LIST THE OBSTACLES TO MAKING THIS CHANGE, AND WHAT YOU CAN DO TO OVERCOME THEM.

Anticipating and developing strategies to overcome obstacles can help you avoid setbacks. List thoughts, behaviors, or excuses that may be barriers to making this change. Also, list external barriers (people, places, things) that may stand in the way of your improvement:

_____

_____

_____

NOTE: If you listed negative thoughts as obstacles to change, refer to the triggers and barriers in Competency 8.

J) DETERMINE AND LIST THOSE THINGS IN YOUR LIFE YOU THAT YOU NEED TO ALTER ABOUT YOURSELF OR YOUR ENVIRONMENT TO MAKE THE CHANGE.

_____

_____

_____

K) WRITE A DAILY ROUTINE FOR CHANGE.

Every day, begin your self-improvement process by doing the following:

1) Visualize the benefits you will get from changing and the negative consequences if you do not change.

2) Review barriers you may encounter and strategies you will use to overcome them.

3) Review the steps listed in the plan you have developed using the Self-Directed Change Planner (A-K, above) then make a list of the things you plan to do today — you can list these items on a 3x5 Daily Action Card you can carry with you throughout the day.

4) Follow through consistently and repetitively on the steps you listed on your Daily Action Card.

5) After the change process begins, become aware of unforeseen things that impede your progress; record these as they come up, along with strategies for countering them.

6) When faced with barriers, counter them.

7) Track your progress by keeping a daily log where you record your daily successes, failures and strategies for overcoming them, insights and lessons learned, and so on (EMPHASIZE YOUR SUCCESSES); if your improvement plan is not working, make appropriate modifications until you "get it right." Successful change may require a number of modifications in your approach.

Summary and Conclusions

To summarize, the contents of this book represent a serious approach to self-improvement and building psychological resilience. It also provides you with a proven process for developing rational thinking and coping and for overcoming irrational habits and addictions.

Although there are many approaches to personal development and self-directed change out there that are helpful and, even though I believe my approach is one of the better ones, rather than argue against other approaches the purpose of this book is to provide the reader—you—with a tried and true recipe for personal and interpersonal development and recovery. I say tried and true because the "recipes" presented here have been tested in my clinics and on large populations around the world and have proven to be universally effective. By universal, I mean these principles have been effective in helping men, women, and children, of different races, from different cultures and religions, around the globe.

As the Turkish Proverb says, "No matter how far you have gone on the wrong road, turn back." The point is that all of us make mistakes, and when we realize we have made one, we need to turn our lives in a different direction.

Unfortunately, many individuals don't have the courage or wherewithal to "turn back." At the same time, many who do have what it takes to change, don't know how to make and sustain the changes required to get back on a good path. Fortunately, the principles, tools, and techniques presented here will help you gain the motivation to change and become your highest and best self.

Once you do gain the courage, knowledge, skills, and tools required to turn your life around, it's important that you get started sooner as is strongly recommended in one of my favorite quotes by Robert Louis Stevenson: "No man can run away from weakness. He must either fight it out or perish. And if that be so… why not now, and where you stand."

Another way to express the point made in this quote is in the form of a question: "Is it better to start thinking and doing things to increase your happiness sooner or later?"

Obviously, if your goal is to increase your happiness now, it's a good idea to start the process as soon as you have developed a specific, realistic plan that will help you navigate the complexities of permanent change and self-improvement. Based on my research and clinical experiences the I have discussed throughout the book, I sincerely believe that understanding the principles and mastering the 13 competencies outlined in this book will take you a long way toward greater happiness and a better life and future. This is because these ideas are based on what leading behavioral and social scientists agree are the most important principles and conditions that must be addressed in an effective self-directed psychological change process that will help you systematically re-engineer or reprogram your beliefs, thoughts, actions, and how you view yourself in a way that helps you become the person you want to become (Cole, 2015; Cole, 2014; Seligman, 2012; Fordyce, 2005; Deiner, 2000; Fishbein, Bandura, Triandis, Kaufer & Becker, 1991; Page, Wrye & Cole, 1986; Cole, Friedman & Bagwell, 1986; Page & Cole, 1985; Cole, 1985; Skinner, 1953).

More specifically, this means that applying the competencies, as prescribed, will help you accomplish the following tasks: understand that everyone who has a healthy brain can learn to live rationally; appreciate the fact that healthy brains have ability to change shape over time (Neuroplasticity), which translates into desirable changes in the brain that result from conscious changes in thinking (i.e., you can use your mind to change your brain for the better); understand that rational living increases happiness and emotional well-being; learn to consistently perceive yourself in a way that increases your happiness and sense of well-being; think in ways that are congruent with rational goals and a rational perception of yourself and your future—a Rational Self Perception (RSP); behave in ways that are consistent with rational goals and a RSP; develop realistic self-improvement plans that work; believe that, in the case of happiness and emotional well-being, it's not what happens to you, or your circumstances, but what you decide to think and do about what happens to you and your circumstances that counts; form a strong positive intention (or make a commitment) to make specific changes; better understand what you can do to build personal resiliency and cope in healthy, rational ways; develop basic skills, such as mental imagery and rehearsal, goal setting, resiliency development, coping, cognitive restructuring, critical thinking, self-discipline, delayed gratification, persistence, planning and problem solving; master monitoring personal status and internal monologues to align your thoughts with your goals; gain the confidence (self-efficacy) you need to do what is required to change; understand intrinsic and extrinsic motivation and how they impact goal-oriented thinking and action; develop positive reinforcement (motivation) for doing what you plan to do; understand how to identify your triggers and overcome your barriers and tendencies to self-sabotage; believe that the advantages of doing what you plan to do outweigh the disadvantages; ensure that what you plan to do and actually end up thinking and doing is, in fact, consistent with your self-image and does not violate your personal standards; understand that setting and striving toward specific goals will give you a greater sense that life has purpose and meaning, and that achieving your personal goals will give you a discernible sense of accomplishment that is often referred to as success—the progressive realization of a worthy ideal. And, finally, this book will provide you with an appreciation for the fact that because setting and achieving goals gives a sense of purpose and feelings of success, it's rational to set and achieve goals. Conversely, not setting goals or setting goals that you don't achieve is irrational. To be rational, a goal must specific, measurable, realistic, and stated in terms of a specific time period. In addition, you must 1) believe you can achieve the goal (have self-efficacy or confidence), and 2) actually be able to achieve it, i.e., have the required knowledge, skills, and abilities. This is because a) it's irrational to assume you can achieve a goal that you don't believe you can achieve, and b) you must become the kind of person who does the kind of thing you plan to do.

I realize all these benefits may seem overwhelming when listed out in this detailed way. At the same time, as was expressed by Menken, "There is always a well-known solution to every human problem—neat, plausible, and wrong." Real, fundamental, lasting change requires much more than the "magical thinking" I once heard a popular self-help guru express when he said to his audience, "You just have to put it out there… and it will happen." It's true, hoping for something good to happen to you and your circumstances is a good thing. However, simply relying on positive thinking is in no way remotely sufficient to what needs to happen to enable you to become the person you want to be. Fortunately, I have provided you with 13 Competencies that move well beyond "Magical Thinking." With positive thinking and some hard work, you can create a positive vision and an attainable plan that will lead to rational lifelong results. With this rational vision of who you want to become, specific goals, an organized action plan, timely decision-making, and persistence, you can take action and achieve successful outcomes.

About the Author

Dr. Galen Cole, PhD, MPH, LPC, DAPA, is a licensed counselor, board certified psychotherapist, and certified hypnotherapist. As a therapist, he provides individual, couple, and family counseling as described at www.galencole.com. He has taught counseling psychology, equine assisted mental health, behavioral and evaluation research, and a number of other counseling and health-related courses at the university level. This includes serving on the undergraduate and/or graduate faculty at Northern Arizona University, Arizona State University, Pennsylvania State University, and Emory University. Dr. Cole has extensive experience practicing what he teaches, including working on staff and as a consultant at numerous clinics, hospitals, and community based organizations; consulting on a number of popular television series; serving as the executive director of a 501(c)(3) foundation; working as an assistant director of the county public health department in Phoenix, Arizona; and working for 23 years as a behavioral scientist and director of research, evaluation, and communication activities in various centers, institutes, and offices at the U.S. Centers for Disease Control and Prevention (CDC) in Atlanta, Georgia. Dr. Cole has also worked at the American Institutes for Research (AIR) as a senior Mental Health Analyst and Thought Leader, and most recently as a Principal Researcher in Mental Health. In 2003, Dr. Cole was appointed by the Governor of Georgia to serve on the Georgia Human Resources (DHR) Board. In this capacity he served as chair of the DHR committee that provided policy guidance to the state Division of Mental Health, Developmental Disabilities, and Addictive Diseases. Dr Cole has served and held leadership positions on a number of boards of directors. This includes serving on the American Psychotherapy Association's Board of Professional Counselors. It also includes serving as the Ethics Chair on the Board of the Georgia Association of Licensed Professional Counselors (GALPC) from 2013-2015. In 2015 he was elected for a term of 3 years to serve as President of the GALPC. Dr. Cole has been a trainer and consultant in the Central Asian Republics, Nigeria, China, Thailand, Kenya, Switzerland, Australia, Peru, Germany, Uganda, and the Middle East, where he has consulted and conducted trainings with the Palestinian Health Authority, the Israeli Ministry of Health, and many other NGOs. He has also provided technical support to a number of prominent international organizations, including the United Nations Children's Fund (UNICEF); the Pan American Health Organization (PAHO); the World Bank; Hollywood, Health and Society (HH&S); and the World Health Organization (WHO). Dr. Cole has published numerous books and scientific papers and made presentations at conferences and training seminars across the world. In recognition of his many accomplishments, Dr. Cole has received distinguished alumni awards from two of the universities he attended. Dr. Cole and his wife, Priscilla, have been married for 40+ years and are the parents of 5 adult children, and grandparents of four grandchildren (Liam, Lilly Rose, Hudson, King) and counting.

References

BURNS, D. D. (1980) Feeling Good: The New Mood Therapy. Avon Books.

CAUTELA, J.R. (1983). The self-control triad: description and clinical applications. Behavior Modification, 7, pp. 299-315.

CAUTELA, J.R., & KASTENBAUM, R. (1967). A reinforcer survey schedule for use in therapy, training, and research. Psychological Reports, 20, pp. 1115-1130.

CHERVIN, D., NOWAK, G., & COLE, G. E. (1999). Using audience research in designing public health initiatives at the federal level. Social Marketing Quarterly, Vo. 5, No. 3, pp. 34-39.

COLE, G.E. (2015). Change You: A Scientific Approach to Recovery from Bad Habits and Addictions. Aphalon Firth Publishers, Atlanta, GA.

COLE, G.E. (2014). Life Script Restructuring: The Neuroplastic Psychology for Rewiring Your Brain and Changing Your Life. Aphalon Firth Publishers, Atlanta, GA.

COLE, G., FRIEDMAN, G., & BAGWELL, M. (1986). A worksite behavioral health education program based on operant conditioning. Occupational Health Nursing, Vol. 24, No. 3, pp. 132-137.

COLE, G. E., WALDRON, S. (2010). Precious Time: The Psychology of Effective Parenting With Parenting Plans. Circle C Publishing, Atlanta, GA.

COLE, G. E. (1999). Advancing The Development and Application of Theory-Based Evaluation in the Practice of Public Health. American Journal of Evaluation, Vol. 20, No. 3, pp. 453-470.

COLE, G. E., LEONARD, B., HAMMOND, S. & FRIDINGER, F. (1998). Using Stages of Behavioral Change constructs to measure the short-term effects of a worksite-based intervention to increase moderate physical activity. Psychological Reports, No. 82, pp. 615-618.

COLE, G. E., POGOSTIN, C., WESTOVER, B., RIOS, N. & COLLIER, C. (1995). Addressing problems in evaluating health-relevant programs through a systematic planning and evaluation model. Risk: Issues in Health, Safety and Environment , Vol. 6, No. 1, pp. 37-57.

COLE, G. E., HOLTGRAVE, D. & RIOS, N. (1993). Systematic development of trans-theoretically based behavioral risk management programs. Risk: Issues in Health, Safety and Environment, Vol. 4, No. 1, pp. 67-93.

COLE, G. E., TIMMRECK, T., PAGE, R. & WOODS, S. (1992). Patterns and prevalence of substance use among Navajo youth. Health Values, Vol. 16, No. 3, pp. 50-57.

COLE, G. E., WALLACE, J. & MCCARTAN, D. (1991). An assessment of the impact of indoor air quality on employee health and satisfaction levels. Occupational Health and Safety, May, pp. 38-51.

COLE, G. E., TUCKER, L. & FRIEDMAN, G. (1990). Relationships among measures of alcohol drinking behavior, life-events and perceived stress. Psychological Reports, Vol. 67, pp. 587-591.

COLE, G. E., TUCKER, L. & FRIEDMAN, G. (1987). Absenteeism data as a measure of cost effectiveness of stress management programs. American Journal of Health Promotion, Vol. 1, No. 4, pp. 12-15.

COLE, G. E., EDDY, J. & FRIEDMAN, G. (1987). A protocol for selecting quality worksite health enhancement services and programs. Occupational Health and Safety, Vol. 56, No. 4, pp. 30-34.

COLE, G. E., TUCKER, L. & FRIEDMAN, G. (1986). Measures of objective and subjective stress by level of income. Psychological Reports, Vol. 59, pp. 139-142.

COLE, G. E., DUNCAN, D. & FRIEDMAN, G. (1986). A systems perspective for hospital based health promotion. Optimal Health, Vol. 3, No. 2, pp. 24-27.

COLE, G. E., FRIEDMAN, G. & BAGWELL, M. (1986). A worksite behavioral health education program based on operant conditioning. Occupational Health Nursing, Vol. 24, No. 3, pp. 132-137.

COLE, G. E. (1985). Life change events as stressors and their relationship to mental health among undergraduate university students. Psychological Reports, Vol. 56, pp. 387-390.

COLE, G. E. (1984). Articulating health promotion into a health services administration curriculum. Health Matrix, Vol. 2, pp. 80-81.

COLE, G. E. (2006). Communication Surveillance: A Case for Message Testing and Information Surveillance in Proactive Risk Communication. G7i Workshop on Proactive Risk Communication (May 2-3, 2006), Berlin, Germany.

COLE, G. & PRUE, C. (1999). CDCynergy: Tool for Strategically Planning Health Communication. 127th Annual Meeting of the American Public Health Association (1999). Chicago, IL.

DEINER, E. (2000). Subjective well-being: The science of happiness and a proposal for a national index. American Psychologist, Vol. 55, No. 1, pp. 34-43

ELLIS, A., HARPER, R. A. & POWERS, M. (1975). A New Guide to Rational Living.

FISHBEIN, M., BANDURA, A., TRIANDIS, H.C., KAUFER, F.H., & BECKER, M.H. (1991). Factors influencing behavior and behavior change. Final report prepared for NIMH theorists workshop, Washington, D.C.

FORDYCE, M. W. (2005) A Review of Research on the Happiness Measures: A Sixty Second Index of Happiness and Mental Health. Social Indicators Research Series, Vol. 26, pp. 373-399.

FREIMUTH, V., COLE, G. E. & KIRBY, S. (2001). Issues in Evaluating Mass-Mediated Health Communication Campaigns in Evaluation in Health Promotion: Principles and Perspectives. WHO Regional Publications, European Series; No 92, pp. 475-492.

GRAHAM, C (2009). Happiness Around the World: The Paradox of Happy Peasants and Miserable Millionaires", OUP Oxford.

GREENBERG, B., SALMON, C., PATEL, D., BECK, V. & COLE, G. E. (2004). Evolution of an Entertainment Education Research Agenda in Cody, M.J., Singhal, A., Sabido, M., & Rogers, E.M. (Eds.) Entertainment-Education Worldwide: History, Research, and Practice. Lawrence Erlbaum Associates, Publishers, Mahwah, NJ.

LALLY, P., VAN JAARSVELD, C. H. M., POTTS, H. W. W., & WARDLE, J. (2010). How are habits formed: Modeling habit formation in the real world. European Journal of Social Psychology, 40, 998-1009.
(http://onlinelibrary.wiley.com/doi/10.1002/ejsp.674/abstract)

LOFLAND, D. (1998). Thought Viruses: Powerful Ways to Change Your Thought Patterns and Get What You Want in Life.

MCMAHON, D. M. (2004). The History of Happiness: 400 B.C. - A.D. 1780, Daedalus Journal, Spring.

PAGE, R., COLE, G. E., & TIMMRECK, T. (1994). Basic Epidemiological Methods and Biostatistics. Jones & Bartlett Publishers, Boston, MA.

PAGE, R. & COLE, G. E. (1992). Demoralization and Living Alone: Outcomes from an Urban Community Study. Psychological Reports, Vol. 70, pp. 275-280.

PAGE, R. & COLE, G. E. (1991). Loneliness and alcoholism risk in late adolescence: A comparative study of adults and adolescents. Adolescence, Vol. 26, No. 104, pp. 925-930.

PAGE, R. & COLE, G. E. (1991). Demographic predictors of self-reported loneliness in adults. Psychological Reports, Vol. 68, pp. 938-945.

PAGE, R. & COLE, G. E. (1986). School health education: A nation at risk. Wellness Perspectives, Vol. 3, No. 2, pp. 37-38.

PAGE, R., WRYE, S. & COLE, G. E. (1986). The role of loneliness in health and wellness. Home Healthcare Nursing, Vol. 4, No. 1, pp. 6-10.

PAGE, R. & COLE, G. E. (1985). Fishbein's Model of Behavioral Intentions: A framework for health education research and development. Int'l Quarterly of Community Health Education, Vol. 5, No. 4, pp. 321-329.

PREMACK, D. (1965). Reinforcement theory. In D. Levin (Ed.), Nebraska

Symposium on Motivation. Lincoln, Nebraska: University of Nebraska Press, pp. 123-180.

RATH, T., & HARTER, J. K. (2010). Wellbeing: The Five Essential Elements. Based on The Gallup-Healthways Well-Being Index.

ROBLES, R., COLON, H., DIAZ, N., MACGOWEN, R., CANCEL, L. & COLE, G. E. (1994). Behavioral risk factors and HIV infection of injection drug users at detoxification clinics in Puerto Rico. International Journal of Epidemiology, Vol. 23, No. 3, pp. 595-601.

SALMON, C., WOOTEN, K., GENTRY, E., COLE, G. E. & KROGER, F. (1996). AIDS Knowledge Gaps: Results from the first decade of the epidemic and implications for future public information efforts. Journal of Health Communication, Vol. 1, No. 2, pp. 141-155.

SELIGMAN, M. E. P. (2012). Flourish: A Visionary New Understanding of Happiness and Well-being.

SELIGMAN, M.E.P. (2004). Can Happiness be Taught? Daedalus Journal, Spring.

SKINNER, B.F. (1953). Science of self-control. New York: Holt, Rinehart & Winston, Inc.

THOMAS, S., COLE, G. E., CROUSE-QUIN, S. & FREIMUTH, V. (2001). A descriptive comparison between blacks and whites on attitudes towards health research and researchers, and perceived knowledge of the Tuskegee Syphilis Study, Social Science and Medicine, Vol. 52, pp. 797-808.

THE SEATTLE AREA HAPPINESS INITIATIVE (2011): The Happiness Initiative All Rights Reserved, http://wholelifewellbeing.com.

TIMMRECK, T. & COLE, G. E. (1989). Health services administration skills: An overlooked need of community health education and health promotion. Health Education, Feb/March, pp. 36-43.

TIMMRECK, T. COLE, G. E., JAMES, G. & BUTTERWORTH, D. (1987). The health education and health promotion movement: A theoretical jungle. Health Education, October/November, pp. 24-28.

TUCKER, L., COLE, G. E. & FRIEDMAN, G. (1987). Stress and serum cholesterol: A study of 7,000 adult males. Health Values, Vol. 2, No. 3, pp. 34-39.

TUCKER, L., COLE, G. E. & FRIEDMAN, G. (1986). Physical fitness: A buffer against stress. Perceptual and Motor Skills, Vol. 63, pp. 955-961.

WALLIS, C. (2005). "Science of Happiness: New Research on Mood, Satisfaction". TIME.

WILKES, M., SRINVASAN, M., COLE, G. E., TARDIF, R., RICHARDSON, L. & PLESCIA, M. (2012). Discussing Uncertainty and Risk in Primary Care: Recommendations of a Multi-Disciplinary CDC Panel Regarding Communication around Prostate Cancer Screening, Journal of General Internal Medicine (in press).

79602877R00102

Made in the USA
Columbia, SC
05 November 2017